Simon Haines
Barbara Stewart

# Cambridge English
# First

# MASTERCLASS

## Workbook Pack with Key

**OXFORD**

UNIVERSITY PRESS

# Contents

1 Appearance and identity 4

2 Talents 10

3 Compulsion 16

4 Roles 22

5 Travel and culture 28

6 The mind 34

7 Free time 40

8 Media 46

9 Around us 52

10 Innovation 58

11 Communication 64

12 Society 70

Key 77

How to use the MultiROM 94

## Listening Part 1

1 🔊 1.1 **You will hear people talking in eight different situations. For questions 1–8, choose the best answer (A, B or C).**

1 You hear two people talking about a recent situation. Where did the situation take place?

   A at a police station

   B at a travel agent's

   C at an airport

2 You hear a message on a telephone answering machine. Why is the speaker calling?

   A to arrange a visit

   B to invite someone somewhere

   C to ask for travel information

3 You hear an athlete talking about his sport. What kind of athlete is he?

   A a sprinter

   B a long jumper

   C a high jumper

4 You hear a footballer being interviewed. How does he feel?

   A anxious

   B angry

   C disappointed

5 You hear a man giving instructions to a group of children. What are the children about to do?

   A run a race

   B perform a play

   C take part in a competition

6 You hear a woman talking on the radio. Why does she think the comedian is so successful?

   A because he is multi-talented

   B because he has an unusual sense of humour

   C because both men and women like him

7 You hear a woman talking to her husband. What does the woman want her husband to do?

   A help more around the house

   B support what she says

   C take more responsibility

8 You hear a man explaining how to do something. What is he explaining?

   A how to toss a pancake

   B how to walk on your hands

   C how to do a party trick

## Vocabulary

➕ *make* or *do*

1 **Complete these sentences with the correct form of *make* or *do*.**

   a It's been a pleasure _____ business with you.

   b You may frighten the birds away if you _____ even the slightest noise.

   c Luckily, the storm didn't _____ any damage to our house.

   d My sister and I take it in turns _____ the cooking.

   e They are currently _____ research into human / computer interaction.

   f I _____ an offer on a motorbike I've wanted to buy for ages.

   g The company is expected to _____ a small profit this year.

# Grammar

## Modal verbs

**1** Complete these sentences with the correct forms of the modal verbs below. In some cases, more than one answer is possible.

> have to    must    need to    should

a You really _____ come and see us soon. We haven't seen you for ages.

b Here's my work phone number in case you _____ get in touch urgently.

c You _____ carry your passport with you at all times. It's the law.

d I had terrible toothache last night, so I _____ make an emergency appointment to see the dentist.

e You _____ take more care of yourself. You're looking very tired.

f If I'm going to help you, I really _____ know more about your situation.

**2** Choose the correct negative verb in these sentences. In one sentence, both are correct.

a In many countries, children *mustn't / don't have to* wear a school uniform.

b You *needn't / mustn't* give me a lift. I can easily catch a bus.

c The last time I crossed the border, I *didn't need to show / needn't have shown* my passport. There was nobody there.

d The arrangements have all been made. There's nothing left to do, so you *don't have to / don't need to* worry about a thing.

e We won tickets for the concert, so we *didn't have to / mustn't* pay anything.

**3** Choose the word or phrase which best completes each sentence.

a In Britain it is _____ for children to attend school between the ages of five and sixteen.

> allowed    compulsory    necessary    possible

b Spectators are reminded that it is _____ to take photographs during the performance.

> banned    forbidden    prevented    restricted

c You _____ leave your bicycle there. It's blocking the footpath.

> can    can't    don't have to    needn't

d In football, only the goalkeeper _____ to touch the ball with his hands.

> can    is allowed    is let    lets

e Unlike some nationalities, British people _____ carry identity cards.

> don't have to    haven't to    mustn't    shouldn't

**4** Read the information in the chart and write sentences describing what young people in Britain are allowed to do, using *can*, *can't* and *be allowed to*.

EXAMPLE

*When you're eighteen, you're allowed to have a tattoo.*

*You can't have a tattoo until you're eighteen.*

| Age | 12 | 13 | 14 | 15 | 16 | 17 | 18 |
|---|---|---|---|---|---|---|---|
| buy pets | ✓ | | | | | | |
| get a part-time job | | ✓ | | | | | |
| leave school | | | | | ✓ | | |
| buy cigarettes | | | | | | | ✓ |
| vote in elections | | | | | | | ✓ |
| become a soldier | | | | | ✓ | | |
| drive a car | | | | | | ✓ | |

# Reading and Use of English Part 5

1 You are going to read a magazine article about Irish folk dancing. For questions 1–6, choose the answer (A, B, C or D) which you think fits best according to the text.

1 What did the stage show *Riverdance* achieve?

A It showed Irish competition dancing at its best.

B It demonstrated how complicated Irish dancing is.

C It presented traditional dances from all over the world.

D It introduced Irish dancing to an international audience.

2 Why do some individual dresses cost so much money?

A They are made of very heavy material.

B The pattern of each dress is different from every other.

C They are made of very expensive material.

D They are created by top designers.

3 What do we find out about the competition judges?

A They are looking for perfection.

B They are sympathetic if a dancer makes a mistake.

C They only watch one dancer at a time.

D They pay great attention to all the dancers.

4 How does the writer compare Irish dancing with other sports?

A She thinks it is more competitive than other sports.

B She thinks performance matters less than in many other sports.

C She thinks experience is more important than in other sports.

D She thinks there is more pressure on the participants than in other sports.

5 What is important about Irish dancing to the dancers themselves?

A the honour of winning competitions

B their beautifully designed costumes

C working hard and making good friends

D the fact that they are representing their country

6 What do people appreciate most about dance competitions?

A the uniqueness of the dancers' costumes

B the teamwork shown by groups of dancers

C the fact that the dancers look beautiful

D the fact that the performers are talented athletes

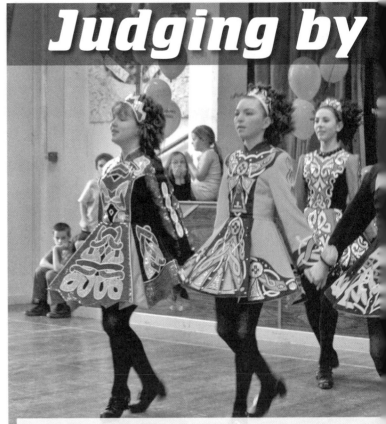

# Judging by

1 Traditional Irish folk dancing, which is well known for its colourful costumes and elaborate steps, has become very glamorous since the stage show *Riverdance* made it recognizable all over the world. What many people do not know about, however, is competition
5 dancing and the importance of appearance in competitions. Appearance, which can include costume, make-up, shoes and posture, can make up 40–50% of the dancer's total score.

Solo competition dresses often run to thousands of dollars because of the intricately embroidered designs which are unique to
10 each dress. The older and more experienced a dancer is, the heavier her make-up and the more elaborate her dress. Dresses, shoes and make-up are all marks of status.

Dancers begin preparing for competitions up to a week in advance by applying fake tan to their legs. Then, for almost an hour
15 and a half before performing, they perfect themselves – applying make-up, attaching wigs, and gluing their socks to their legs to prevent them from falling down. It seems incredible that the couple of hours a dancer spends preparing for a competition are almost equal in points to the months, or even years, that she spends
20 perfecting and memorizing complicated steps.

In competition, dancers will perform different steps in a line of a dozen or more dancers. A judge will watch several dancers at once, but if the judge perceives a single imperfection in the dancer's appearance or in her performance, he will move on to watch a
25 better dancer. If a dancer cannot catch and hold the attention of the judge, she has no chance of winning a medal or even a place.

# appearances

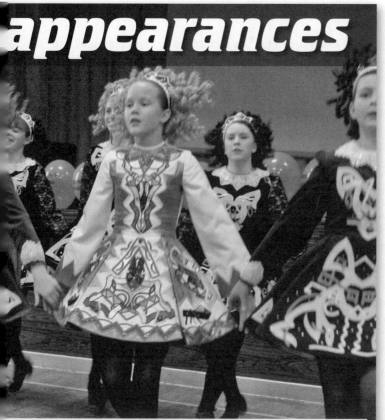

The pressure this inspires can affect a dancer negatively because she is consequently more worried about what people think of her, instead of just doing her best. By emphasizing costume and
30 appearance generally, competitive Irish dance has become part of the cut-throat show business industry. Irish dance instructors often give this advice: 'Whatever happens, don't cry; it will ruin your make-up.' Pressure to perform is a key element in any sport, and is often a positive factor in an athlete's overall experience. In modern-day
35 competitive Irish dance, however, the pressure of appearance can have a very negative impact on a dancer's career.

Nonetheless, when asked what Irish dancing means to them, most dancers will answer 'close friends and hard work'. Though almost half of a dancer's score is determined by her appearance,
40 the aspects of the sport that don't receive points, such as sportsmanship, friendships, tradition, community and artistry, still remain of the greatest importance. These are the central ideas that are represented in Irish dance. In fact, the designs on a solo dress have their origins in these ideas: those Celtic designs were created
45 to represent certain symbols, such as unity and friendship.

Because of the very visual nature of dance, external beauty, form, and expression obviously have a large place in the sport. And, although the sheer complexity of costume preparation may seem intimidating, in the drama of competitive Irish dance, it is legitimate. Visually, the
50 true attraction of dance competition is the athleticism and skill of the dancers, both as individuals and as teams. In the end, the emphasis on appearance will only negatively affect the sport if it becomes more important than the other aspects of competitive Irish dance.

## Grammar

**1 Choose the correct form of the verb to complete these sentences.**

**a** Can I ring you back? *I drive / I'm driving* to work at the moment.

**b** *You always tell / You're always telling* me what TV programmes I should watch. It's really annoying.

**c** Do you know who this hat *belongs / is belonging* to?

**d** Normally *I work / I'm working* at home, but this week *I travel / I'm travelling* all over the country.

**e** *I don't usually eat / I'm not usually eating* meat, but this beef *tastes / is tasting* delicious.

**f** Did I tell you that my sister *expects / is expecting* a baby?

**2 Complete this email with the correct form of the verb in brackets. All verbs should be in either the present simple or the present continuous tense. Sometimes both tenses are possible.**

Rome!

**To:** Ed

**Subject:** Rome!

Hi Ed,

I told you I was going to Rome, didn't I? Well, I'm actually here now. It's a fantastic city. The sun **(a)** _____ (shine) every day and it never **(b)** _____ (seem) to rain. The people are very friendly, and most of them **(c)** _____ (speak) English very well. I **(d)** _____ (try) to speak Italian, but I **(e)** _____ (know) I **(f)** _____ (make) lots of mistakes.

I **(g)** _____ (spend) a week here with some friends I'm at university with, and we **(h)** _____ (visit) as many of the ancient sites as we can. I'm sure everyone **(i)** _____ (know) what the Colosseum is like because they've seen it on TV or in films, but it **(j)** _____ (look) even more impressive in real life. It's a huge tourist attraction.

I'll give you a ring as soon as I **(k)** _____ (get) back. We **(l)** _____ (leave) here on Saturday morning and **(m)** _____ (arrive) back in London just after lunch.

Hope all's well.

Polly

# Writing Part 1

**1** **The paragraphs of this sample essay are not in the correct order. Read the essay and put the five paragraphs in the correct order. Do not try to choose the correct words yet.**

☐ It is clear that for some of these people, such experiments with appearance are successful; **(a)** *but / however* things can go seriously wrong. Unfortunately, **(b)** *this / such* can cause great unhappiness and can even ruin people's lives.

☐ It seems that the majority of operations are on people **(c)** *who / which* are simply unhappy with the way they look. They believe that altering their physical appearance will increase their confidence or make them more attractive to other people. They hope surgery will make it easier for them to make friends or to get a good job.

☐ **(d)** *They / There* have been many recent reports about cosmetic surgery operations that have gone wrong. When I heard about these, I wondered why so many people choose to have these operations.

☐ **(e)** *To / In* conclude, I would suggest that everyone considering cosmetic surgery should first receive honest medical advice and be warned about the risks involved.

☐ **(f)** *It / There* is no doubt that some cosmetic operations are necessary for medical or psychological reasons, **(g)** *by / for* example for patients who have been involved in serious accidents. **(h)** *However / But*, it is clear from the number of operations conducted every year that most 'patients' are not in **(i)** *this / the* category.

**2** **Now choose the correct words in italics in a–i above.**

# Reading and Use of English Part 1

**1** **For questions 1–8, read the text below and decide which answer (A, B, C or D) best fits each gap. There is an example at the beginning (0).**

Tweetie de Leon-Gonzalez **(0)** *broke* into the competitive world of modelling at the age of 14. Advertisers **(1)** _____ notice, but she was not easily **(2)** _____ from getting her education. She accepted modelling projects but made **(3)** _____ these were only at weekends. With a discipline that would make any parent proud, this hard-working student finished high school and then **(4)** _____ a university degree in philosophy.

After graduating, Tweetie went job-hunting, but modelling projects continued to **(5)** _____ her way, until her days were all booked up. It was only after **(6)** _____ a competition that she decided to take **(7)** _____ modelling as a profession. As well as earning the respect of other models, she established solid friendships throughout her career. Yet at the height of her popularity, she turned her back on the glamour of the fashion world because she was finding modelling less and less **(8)** _____ . She said it was beginning to feel more like work than enjoyment.

| | | | | |
|---|---|---|---|---|
| **0** | **A** threw | **B** started | **C** broke | **D** launched |
| **1** | **A** took | **B** got | **C** made | **D** saw |
| **2** | **A** disturbed | **B** distracted | **C** interested | **D** interrupted |
| **3** | **A** definite | **B** careful | **C** clear | **D** sure |
| **4** | **A** awarded | **B** held | **C** won | **D** earned |
| **5** | **A** come | **B** find | **C** go | **D** make |
| **6** | **A** taking | **B** gaining | **C** winning | **D** going |
| **7** | **A** on | **B** to | **C** up | **D** in |
| **8** | **A** rewarding | **B** popular | **C** agreeable | **D** entertaining |

# Vocabulary

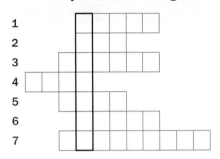

**Body words and seeing verbs**

1 2 3 4 5 6 7

**1  Read the definitions and fill in the missing words.**

1 Look at something for a long time without moving your eyes. (5 letters)

2 The part of your foot that you can stub. (3 letters)

3 See / spot / become conscious of. (6 letters)

4 The part of your hand that a fortune-teller reads. (4 letters)

5 Look lovingly at someone. (4 letters)

6 Move on your hands and knees like a baby. (5 letters)

7 The parts of your body that you shrug. (9 letters)

**2  Find the missing vertical word in the crossword which is a more formal word for *tummy*.**

**Adverbs**

**3  Choose the correct adverb in these sentences. Check in your dictionary if necessary.**

a I didn't realize the path was so icy until I fell *flat / flatly* on my back.

b Ever since the accident, I haven't been able to move my arm *free / freely*.

c Every night, several hundred people sleep *rough / roughly* in the city centre.

d We all thought he was asleep, but when we looked closely at him, his eyes were *wide / widely* open.

e I haven't been to the cinema *late / lately*. Are there any good films on?

**➕ Body idioms**

**4  Choose the correct part of the body from the list to complete the idioms in *italics* in these sentences. There are two words that you do not need to use. Check in your dictionary if necessary.**

| arm | back | feet | finger | hair | head | legs | neck | nose | tongue |

a Her father says 'yes' to everything she asks for. *She can twist him round her little* _____ .

b I wouldn't get too friendly with John if I were you. He's quite likely to *stab you in the* _____ .

c I can't remember her name. It's driving me mad – it's *on the tip of my* _____ .

d By the time children are sixteen or seventeen, they've learned to *stand on their own two* _____ .

e I'd *give my right* _____ for a ticket to the Olympic Games.

f As usual, I've got too much work to do, but I'm just about managing to *keep my* _____ *above water*.

g The person sitting behind me was a real *pain in the* _____ . He talked all the way through the film.

h I watched a horror film at the cinema last night. It was really frightening. It made my _____ *stand on end*.

## Reading and Use of English Part 7

1 You are going to read a newspaper article about a child genius. For questions 1–10, choose from the sections (A–D). The sections may be chosen more than once.

**Which paragraph**

| | |
|---|---|
| says that the writer found it hard to establish rules? | 1 |
| suggests that the writer controlled how Leo spent his leisure time? | 2 |
| describes an incident which shocked the writer? | 3 |
| gives an example of Leo's inventiveness? | 4 |
| states that the writer believed some people thought he wasn't strict enough with Leo? | 5 |
| refers to Leo's enquiring mind? | 6 |
| gives examples of Leo's stubbornness? | 7 |
| states that the writer finds parenting Leo difficult but worthwhile? | 8 |
| suggests that the writer is confident that Leo will succeed in life? | 9 |
| says that finding the right environment for Leo was key to his development? | 10 |

# CHILD GENIUS

*Martin Buckley writes about his son Leo, a finalist on the TV series 'Child Genius'.*

**A**

1 My 11-year-old son Leo is a finalist in Channel 4's 'Child Genius' competition. For me, it caps a decade spent learning how to raise a child whose intellect and independence of spirit simply aren't ordinary. It has been rewarding, but it hasn't always 5 been easy. I was struck by Leo's curiosity and independence of thought almost as soon as he could speak. When I told little Leo something, he would hungrily analyze it and respond with a penetrating question. He learned to play Monopoly at four and was soon beating me; at six, he had read the *Odyssey*. He would 10 do jigsaw puzzles without the pictures – because it was more challenging. In fact, for every game he played, he would make up new rules, ones that would make the games harder.

**B**

Leo's IQ was tested on his 11th birthday. It scored him in the top 0.01 per cent of his age group. So yes, he is bright. I think I only 15 fully admitted that to myself after I saw those results. Not having other children, I had no real way of measuring Leo's intelligence. And, also, I have to admit that part of me just wanted a standard kid. Every parent wants their child to socialize well and make friends, not to be a genius and potentially difficult. Discipline was 20 challenging. Explaining to Leo that he needed to sit in a given place, eat a given meal, follow a given routine, he would invariably ask, 'Why?'. And, often, he'd refuse. By the time he was four, it was sometimes hard to tell if he was wildly creative, or merely wild. I felt isolated, because many parents and teachers assumed 25 that Leo was allowed to do just as he liked. The opposite was true. We worked daily to impose routines. But Leo was reluctant to go along with anything just because he was asked to.

**C**

There are of course other downsides to having a very bright child. Not least of these is dealing with the education system. I've seen 30 state schools that are content to be of average standard, and expensive private schools with equally average teachers that don't make allowances for students who have different needs, which I find alarming. I will never forget the ignorant teacher who, in my hearing, patronized my six-year-old when he referred 35 to Shakespeare as a poet. 'He wrote prose,' she snapped. Eventually, we found the right school for him. His frustration has gone, he has matured, he has strong friendships, and his grades are mainly 'A's. At last, he's just an intelligent, appropriately stimulated child, and achieving his potential.

**D**

40 'Child Genius' has very much cast me in the role of the pushy parent, but I would argue that I have simply been discriminating. Leo has seen little live television in his life; instead, good stuff on DVDs and as many books as he has wanted. At six, he was reading versions of the classics written for teenagers, and last 45 week we watched *Coriolanus* together. Shakespeare's language was not a barrier for him. This September, Leo goes to a highly academic secondary school, and he plans to go to university. He's strong in maths and English, and a keen actor. What will he become, I wonder: a barrister, a doctor, a journalist? I tell him he 50 can be anything he wants to be, and I believe it. The programme has confirmed my belief that raising a really bright child is a task society neither really understands nor supports.

# Vocabulary

**Adjective prefixes: *extra, hyper, over, under***

**1** Complete the sentences with an appropriate prefix + adjective from the list below.

| critical | curricular | dressed | grown | ordinary | qualified | valued |
| --- | --- | --- | --- | --- | --- | --- |

**a** Hospital staff have gone on strike, complaining that they are _____ and underpaid.

**b** The party invitation said 'smart-casual', but I don't think either Tom or Sophie read it. He was _____ as he turned up in a tuxedo, and Sophie was _____ as she arrived in a pair of scruffy jeans.

**c** No one had lived in the house for years and the garden was really _____ .

**d** My favourite _____ activity at school was drama.

**e** My English teacher at school was _____ . She pointed out every single mistake I made and I got discouraged as a result.

**f** Winning the championship seven times in a row was an _____ achievement.

**g** When my friend Josh applied for a job stacking shelves in a local supermarket, he was told he was _____ for the job. Next time, he's not going to say he's a graduate.

**⊕ Phrasal verbs with *set***

**2** Replace the verbs in *italics* in these sentences with the correct form of *set* and one of these words.

| back | off | out | (something) on | up |
| --- | --- | --- | --- | --- |

**a** A cat which got into the house through an open window *made the burglar alarm ring*.

**b** We'd better *leave* early tomorrow. We've got a long way to travel.

**c** Recently more and more people have been *starting* their own internet companies.

**d** The police *made their dogs attack* the bank robbers as they tried to escape.

**e** The terrible rainstorms we've had recently have *delayed the house-building programme* by several months.

**f** I'm going to write to the principal *expressing my ideas* for improvements to the school.

# Grammar

**can, be able to, manage, succeed**

1 Choose the correct alternative in *italics* in these sentences. In which two sentences are both options correct?

   a How long *could you / have you been able to* drive?

   b I *can't / 'm not able to* understand a word he's saying, can you?

   c The teacher told me he *couldn't / didn't manage to* correct my essay because he *couldn't read / didn't succeed in reading* my writing.

   d Has your brother *managed to / been able to* find a job?

   e I *could / was able to* beat you at chess any day of the week.

   f A tall man stood in front of me at the concert, so I *couldn't / wasn't able to* see a thing.

   g I *can't / 'm not able to* believe it. I got an 'A' in maths!

   h Fortunately, they *could / were able to* rescue the children from the burning building.

2 Complete these questions with an appropriate form of *can* or *be able to*. In which sentences are both options correct?

   a ＿＿＿＿＿＿ come to my party on Saturday, or have you made other plans? (you)

   b ＿＿＿＿＿＿ speak Spanish before you went to live in Spain? (you)

   c ＿＿＿＿＿＿ ever ＿＿＿＿＿＿ do everything people do, do you think? (robots)

   d ＿＿＿＿＿＿ get the sofa in if we took the door off? (we)

   e ＿＿＿＿＿＿ find out Richard's new phone number yet? (David)

   f My jeans are torn. ＿＿＿＿＿＿ repair them? (you)

   g ＿＿＿＿＿＿ picked us up if we'd asked you sooner? (you)

3 Complete these sentences with the correct form of *can*. If it is not possible to use *can*, use the correct form of *be able to*. You may need to use the negative.

   a When you give your speech at tomorrow's conference, nobody ＿＿＿＿＿＿ understand you unless you speak more clearly.

   b I'm afraid I ＿＿＿＿＿＿ go to the party. I was busy on Saturday.

   c Janet ＿＿＿＿＿＿ read before she was three years old. I think that's amazing!

   d They ＿＿＿＿＿＿ eat any more. They were full.

   e Despite the delay, the passengers ＿＿＿＿＿＿ get their connecting flights.

   f I ＿＿＿＿＿＿ tell Darren yet, but I will as soon as I see him.

   g Sara ＿＿＿＿＿＿ walk for a long time after the accident. She had to use a wheelchair.

   h When the chip pan caught fire, John ＿＿＿＿＿＿ put the fire out with a wet cloth.

4 Complete these sentences with *can, be able to, manage* or *succeed* in an appropriate form. You may need to use the negative.

   a That's as fast as I can run. I ＿＿＿＿＿＿ run any faster even if I tried.

   b Despite setting off late, Karen ＿＿＿＿＿＿ to catch the train.

   c Even if the fire fighters had arrived sooner, they ＿＿＿＿＿＿ saved the building.

   d I'd like to ＿＿＿＿＿＿ play a musical instrument.

   e He ＿＿＿＿＿＿ play tennis since he hurt his back.

   f The high jumper finally ＿＿＿＿＿＿ in clearing the bar on his third attempt.

# Reading and Use of English Part 3

1 For questions 1–8, read the text below. Use the word given in capitals at the end of some of the lines to form a word that fits in the gap in the same line. There is an example at the beginning (0).

# CHAMELEONS

| | |
|---|---|
| Chameleons, a (0) _____variety_____ of tree-living lizard, are found in Africa, Madagascar, Asia, | VARY |
| Arabia and Southern Europe. They are unusual in their (1) _____ with their bulging eyes, | APPEAR |
| which move (2) _____ , and their long curled tail, which can be twisted around branches to | DEPEND |
| increase their grip. The chameleon's eyesight is exceptional for a reptile: its 360-degree | |
| vision makes it highly (3) _____ at hunting prey and spotting predators. | EFFECT |
| | |
| Chameleons will eat everything, from leaves and fruits to insects. When they spot an | |
| insect, their long tongue, which has a (4) _____ substance at its end, will shoot out | STICK |
| faster than the human eye can see. | |
| | |
| Contrary to popular (5) _____ , most chameleons do not change colour to blend in with | BELIEVE |
| their (6) _____ , although some species are able to do so. Colour change comes about | SURROUND |
| because of changes in light or temperature, or because they are angry or frightened. | |
| Today, many chameleon species are (7) _____ because of pollution and the | DANGER |
| (8) _____ of their natural habitat. | DESTROY |

# Vocabulary

● Nouns from phrasal verbs

1 It is often possible to form nouns from phrasal verbs. Complete these sentences with an appropriate noun from the list below.

| breakout | breakthrough | hold-up | let-down | outbreak |
|---|---|---|---|---|
| takeaway | take-off | turnout | | |

a In the triple jump, your speed just before _____ determines the height you achieve.

b There was a _____ at the main branch of Barclays Bank in Swindon last Tuesday. Three armed men got away with several thousand pounds.

c There was a good _____ for the cup final. The stadium was full.

d I don't want to cook tonight. Let's get an Indian _____ .

e There was a mass _____ from Barlinnie prison last night. Fifty prisoners managed to overpower the guards and escape.

f The holiday was a real _____ . We were very disappointed with the hotel, and the weather was awful.

g The discovery of penicillin was an important medical _____ .

h There has been another _____ of typhoid in the area.

13

## Listening Part 2

1 🔊 1.2 You will hear a journalist called Richard Prior talking about the time he met the autistic savant Daniel Tammet. For questions 1–10, complete the sentences with a word or short phrase.

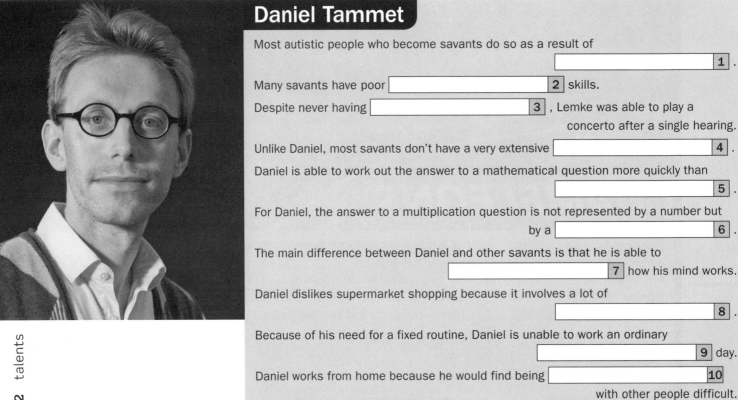

### Daniel Tammet

Most autistic people who become savants do so as a result of _____ [1] .

Many savants have poor _____ [2] skills.

Despite never having _____ [3] , Lemke was able to play a concerto after a single hearing.

Unlike Daniel, most savants don't have a very extensive _____ [4] .

Daniel is able to work out the answer to a mathematical question more quickly than _____ [5] .

For Daniel, the answer to a multiplication question is not represented by a number but by a _____ [6] .

The main difference between Daniel and other savants is that he is able to _____ [7] how his mind works.

Daniel dislikes supermarket shopping because it involves a lot of _____ [8] .

Because of his need for a fixed routine, Daniel is unable to work an ordinary _____ [9] day.

Daniel works from home because he would find being _____ [10] with other people difficult.

## Vocabulary

**Comparative and superlative adjectives and adverbs**

1 Complete these sentences with the comparative or superlative form of an appropriate adjective or adverb from this list. You can use one of the words twice.

| bad | carefully | clearly | clever | expensive | fat |
|-----|-----------|---------|--------|-----------|-----|
| good | heavy | high | superstitious | | |

a She's the _____ person I've ever met. This morning, on the way to college, she refused to walk under a ladder.

b My suitcase is _____ than yours. I can hardly lift mine.

c That's the _____ car we've looked at so far. We couldn't possibly afford to buy it.

d I can see much _____ now that I've cleaned my glasses.

e I'm _____ than I was this time last year – I must go on a diet.

f Women drive _____ than men – that's why they have fewer accidents.

g There's no doubt that she's the _____ student in the class. She always gets the _____ marks in tests.

h He's a brilliant maths teacher. He explains things much _____ than any teacher I've ever had.

i I hope the weather doesn't get _____ – we're going on holiday on Saturday.

j That was the _____ film I've seen in a long time – I thought it was even _____ than this year's Oscar winner.

# Writing Part 2 – Letter / email

1 **Read this email, which was written in response to someone asking for advice about taking up a new sport. Replace the underlined words and phrases (a–p) with more appropriate informal words and phrases from this list.**

| | | | | | | |
|---|---|---|---|---|---|---|
| all the best | for a while | free | fun | good to hear from you | hard | |
| hope this helps | make up your mind | more than happy | perhaps | quite | | |
| so | start | suits | till | to start with | | |

> **Advice**
>
> **To:** John
>
> **Subject:** Advice
>
> Hello! **(a)** <u>I was very pleased to receive your email</u>. I'd be **(b)** <u>delighted</u> to give you some advice. **(c)** <u>First of all</u>, you need to **(d)** <u>decide</u> whether you want to do a team sport or an individual sport. Team sports are more **(e)** <u>enjoyable</u>, but you would need to commit yourself to being **(f)** <u>available</u> on particular days and at particular times. That might be **(g)** <u>problematic</u> for you as you are always so busy. **(h)** <u>For this reason,</u> **(i)** <u>it may be that</u> an individual sport would be more suitable for you.
>
> As you haven't done any exercise **(j)** <u>in some time</u>, I'd suggest you **(k)** <u>begin</u> with something that isn't too difficult. I'd recommend either jogging or swimming. Neither of them is expensive and you can do them at a time which **(l)** <u>is convenient for</u> you. You can go for a jog before or after work and swimming pools are usually open from early morning **(m)** <u>until</u> **(n)** <u>relatively</u> late. The advantage of doing either of these sports is that you can start off gently at your own pace and increase this as you get fitter.
>
> Anyway, **(o)** <u>I hope I have been of some assistance</u>.
>
> **(p)** <u>Yours sincerely,</u>
>
> George

2 **Look at the underlined formal words and phrases below. Then choose the more appropriate words or phrases to complete the sentences.**

a <u>It gives me great pleasure</u> to *let you know / inform you* that you have been chosen to *receive / get* a special prize, and a cheque in your name is waiting *for you to claim / to be claimed* now.

b <u>All the items are available for order using the enclosed form.</u> *Simply write / You just need to write* the code numbers of *the items you want / your chosen items* in the boxes.

c <u>We would be most grateful if you could return the completed questionnaire</u> *at your convenience / whenever you have time*.

d <u>Your rooms have been allocated</u> and *they will be reserved / we will reserve them* for you. Please *let us know / notify us* of any changes in advance *to avoid additional charges / so that we do not need to charge you extra*.

e <u>Take your completed form,</u> *photographs / photos* and *the documents you had to bring / required documents* to any post office and *they will give you your identity card on the spot / your identity card will be issued immediately*.

## Vocabulary

**Phrasal verbs with *give*** 1 Replace the verbs in *italics* in these sentences with the correct form of *give* and one of these words.

| away | back | in | out | up |
|------|------|-----|-----|-----|

a When are you going to *return* the CD you borrowed from me last year?

b At the beginning of the exam, the teacher *distributed* the question papers.

c I've tried not to play so many video games, but I'm hooked – I just can't *stop doing it*.

d They are *letting you have* a T-shirt *free* with every CD you buy.

e My little brother realized he wasn't going to win the game, so he *admitted defeat*.

## Grammar

**Habitual actions** 1 In each of these sets of three sentences, two sentences have a similar meaning and one has a different meaning. Put a cross (✗) next to the sentence with a different meaning.

a 1 I always used to walk to school.

   2 I would always walk to school.

   3 I've always walked to school.

b 1 I used to get up early.

   2 I am used to getting up early.

   3 I am accustomed to getting up early.

c 1 I usually check my emails before I get up.

   2 Normally, I'd check my emails before I got up.

   3 Normally, I'll check my emails before I get up.

2 Choose the correct words in italics to complete these sentences.

a I lived in Africa for nearly five years, but I *never got used to / was never used to* the heat.

b I *got used to smoking / used to smoke*, but I gave up nearly three years ago.

c Even though they are only three years old, the twins *are used to getting dressed / used to get dressed* themselves.

d People from other countries *get used to driving / are used to driving* on the left quite quickly when they come to Britain.

e Where *did you use to live / were you used to living* before you moved to New York?

# Listening Part 4

1 🔊 1.3 You will hear part of a radio interview with a woman called Maggie Lyons, who is talking about gambling addiction. For questions 1–7, choose the best answer (A, B or C).

1 Which of these best describes Maggie's current situation?

 A Her addiction is not as serious as in the past.

 B She is receiving advice about how stop gambling.

 C She is no longer addicted to gambling.

2 Why does Maggie describe how she got into gambling as 'innocent'?

 A She didn't start by gambling large amounts of money.

 B She didn't really understand what she was getting into.

 C She didn't believe that gambling could become addictive.

3 Why did nobody advise Maggie to stop gambling?

 A Nobody even suspected her addiction.

 B They didn't realize she was gambling large sums of money.

 C She had made sure that nobody knew she was gambling.

4 How did she obtain more money when her own started to run out?

 A She took out a bank loan.

 B Her father lent her some.

 C She sold her car.

5 What did the counsellor suggest Maggie should do to help herself?

 A Find an alternative way of spending her time.

 B Change her behaviour slowly over time.

 C Join a gambling addicts group.

6 What happened to Maggie after she saw the addiction counsellor?

 A She pretended she had got over her addiction.

 B She found it easier to stop gambling than she had imagined.

 C She developed new interests.

7 How do the addicts Maggie works with react to her methods?

 A They all manage to stop gambling.

 B Most of them change their behaviour in some way.

 C Some people react against her methods.

# Grammar

**Countable and uncountable nouns**

1 **Choose the correct word or phrase to complete these sentences.**

 a I have little *experience / experiences* of shift work.

 b Every time I leave the flat, I make sure I turn all the *light / lights* off.

 c I can sleep through most kinds of *noise / noises*, but not car alarms.

 d How *many times / much time* did you spend writing that essay?

 e When I graduate, I'd like to get into *language / languages* teaching.

 f After his operation, the doctor gave him some special *exercise / exercises* to do.

 g Unfortunately, we don't have enough *room / rooms* for a piano in our apartment.

2 **Complete sentences a–g with the correct word from the list. Sometimes more than one answer is possible.**

| bit | box | item | piece | sheet | stroke | word |
|-----|-----|------|-------|-------|--------|------|

 a When I was ten, my father gave me a / an _____ of advice I've never forgotten.

 b Could I borrow a / an _____ of paper to write notes on, please?

 c That was a / an _____ of luck – someone found my phone and took it to reception.

 d I didn't mean to upset you. It was just a / an _____ of fun.

 e That's a lovely _____ of furniture. Do you know how old it is?

 f Do you have a / an _____ of matches I can borrow to light the fire, please?

 g Tonight, the young pianist will be playing a / an _____ of music by Chopin.

1  You are going to read a magazine article which explains some of the reasons why people collect things. Six sentences have been removed from the article. Choose from the sentences A–G the one which fits each gap (1–6). There is one extra sentence which you do not need to use.

# Why do we collect?

1 People have been collecting things for centuries. Their collections range from rare baseball cards worth thousands of dollars to beautiful, brightly-coloured oriental jewels that glisten in display cases, showing their owner's wealth. **1 ⬚**

5 Even with a valuable collection, it isn't often that a collector sells up and claims the money. Why, then, would someone put so much time and effort into amassing a valuable collection?

Terry Shoptaugh, from Minnesota State University 10 Moorhead, can shine some light on why people collect. In an article, he offers the idea that collecting is based on a need to inspire recollection. **2 ⬚** 'We use keepsakes to stimulate memory, especially to trigger happy memories,' Shoptaugh writes. 'But even if memory cannot be relied 15 upon to faithfully reproduce the past, it remains vital to our understanding of the past.' This may explain why people collect unattractive, old war memorabilia in an effort to remember the romantic aspects of war while not forgetting the true horror of such times.

20 Anthropologist Marjorie Akin is also an expert on collecting. She shares Shoptaugh's idea that people collect for a connection to the past and memories. She writes: 'Objects can connect the collector to the historic, valued past.' Akin also gives four other reasons why people collect. The first 25 is to satisfy a sense of personal order and beauty. Some collect to please personal tastes. **3 ⬚** Another reason is the collector's need for completeness. Akin says she has seen people cry out with relief once their collection is complete.

Kim Herzinger, an English professor and an avid collector, 30 provides yet another explanation for our obsession with collecting. Herzinger says: 'Collecting is a way of dealing with a feeling of incompleteness that many people feel in childhood.' He adds, however, that collecting is also a passion. **4 ⬚** Herzinger also believes that it's important for 35 collectors to maintain a sense of control over their collection. **5 ⬚** To avoid this, the collector narrows the field from baseball cards to, for example, the New York Yankees cards.

Herzinger admits that while the collection brings much joy to the collector, there will always be disappointment. 'I once 40 had a very good friend, a record collector, who was showing me around his collection of valuable American jazz records. **6 ⬚** Many people feel they have a special bond with their collection and can't help feeling frustrated if no one else seems to appreciate it as much as they do.'

45 A simpler explanation for the popularity of collecting as a hobby is suggested by Kurt Kuersteiner, who says, 'I believe the main reason people collect things is a basic interest in the topic.' Can it really be that simple?

**A** After showing me his favourite items, he became silent, apparently disappointed with my lack of response.

**B** And, like most similar obsessions, it lets you live in another world for a while.

**C** Despite this, she believes that some people collect for money and profit.

**D** However, more collections consist of oddities that have nothing more than sentimental value for the collector.

**E** In other words, people collect in an effort to remember and relive the past.

**F** Others collect items that are weird or unusual to show their individualism.

**G** To collect every baseball card would be impossible, leaving the collector with a feeling of always being overwhelmed.

# Vocabulary

**Word formation**  **1** This table contains verbs and nouns from the reading text. Complete the table with the missing words. The first one is done as an example.

| | Noun | Verb |
|---|---|---|
| **a** | collection | *collect* |
| **b** | _____ | inspire |
| **c** | relief | _____ |
| **d** | _____ | explain |
| **e** | _____ | provide |
| **f** | _____ | satisfy |
| **g** | disappointment | _____ |
| **h** | _____ | appreciate |
| **i** | response | _____ |
| **j** | _____ | believe |

**➕ Order of adjectives in front of nouns**  **2** Read the information in the box. Then complete these sentences a–e with the adjectives in brackets in the correct order.

> *... collections range from baseball cards to beautiful, brightly-coloured oriental jewels (opinion + colour + origin)*
>
> *This may explain why people collect unattractive, old war memorabilia (opinion + age)*
>
> *... his collection of valuable American jazz records (quality + origin)*
>
> **The normal order of adjectives is:**
>
> **opinion > size > quality > age > shape > colour > origin > material > purpose**
>
> **But remember, we rarely use more than three adjectives together in front of a noun.**

**a** We saw several _____ statues in the museum. (Roman / old / huge)

**b** The whole team were wearing _____ baseball caps. (green / cotton / unusual)

**c** I work in a _____ office building. (tall / modern / beautiful)

**d** One room of the exhibition was full of _____ photographs. (black and white / large / square)

**e** I've just bought myself a _____ digital camera. (brand new / Japanese / tiny)

19

## Reading and Use of English Part 2

1 For questions 1–8, read the text below and think of the word which best fits each gap. Use only one word in each gap. There is an example at the beginning (0).

### Blogaholics

The word 'blog' is short for 'weblog' and is a frequently-updated internet journal that is intended for **(0)** _the_ general public to read. Blogs are popular because they give their authors, bloggers, **(1)** _____ own voice on the internet. It's a place **(2)** _____ ordinary people can share interests – whether through a political commentary, a personal diary, **(3)** _____ a list of links to favourite websites.

Professional as **(4)** _____ as amateur journalists often use blogs to publish breaking news, while personal bloggers may prefer to share their inner thoughts **(5)** _____ the rest of the world.

For many people, blogging is just a hobby, but for others it can become an obsession. Bloggers **(6)** _____ fall into this group can feel compelled to write several times a day and become anxious if something prevents them **(7)** _____ blogging. As with other addicts, these people spend more and more of their time on their obsession and may end **(8)** _____ neglecting their families, their friends and their jobs.

## Vocabulary

**Adverbs** 1 List these adverbs under the correct headings.

| absolutely | always | completely | dangerously | deliberately | especially |
|---|---|---|---|---|---|
| even | hard | interestingly | luckily | occasionally | only | rarely | sensitively |
| sometimes | surprisingly | totally | unfortunately | very |

Adverbs of manner: _____ , _____ , _____ , _____

Comment adverbs: _____ , _____ , _____ , _____

Focusing adverbs: _____ , _____ , _____

Frequency adverbs: _____ , _____ , _____ , _____

Adverbs of degree: _____ , _____ , _____ , _____

2 Rewrite these sentences using an appropriate adverb from the list in **1** in the correct position. Sometimes more than one adverb can be used.

a I only caught my train because it was a few minutes late – that was lucky.
   _Luckily, I caught my train because it was a few minutes late._

b I go to the theatre from time to time if there's something good on.
   _____

c My brother was stopped by the police because he wasn't driving safely.
   _____

d I hate long road journeys. I hate them most in the winter when the roads are icy.
   _____

e My sister passed her driving test first time. That surprised everyone.
   _____

f When I was four, I broke my brother's favourite toy. It was not an accident.
   _____

g That was a terrible fire. The house was destroyed – there's nothing left of it.
   _____

# Writing Part 2 – Article

1  Here are eight subjects for magazine articles. Find a suitable title A–H for each subject, then choose one of the 'first lines' a–h. The first one is done as an example.

| Subjects | Title | First line |
|---|---|---|
| 1  changes to my town in the last five years | A | e |
| 2  clothes you like wearing | | |
| 3  an ideal holiday | | |
| 4  the worries of today's youth | | |
| 5  superstitions in the modern world | | |
| 6  the future of money | | |
| 7  a school subject you found useful | | |
| 8  methods of relaxing | | |

**Titles**

A  That's progress – or is it?

B  Ways to chill out

C  Paradise on earth

D  Today's teenagers – their hopes and fears

E  Comfort or looks?

F  A lesson worth learning

G  Tomorrow is plastic

H  We can't go today – it's Friday 13th

**First lines**

a  I hate coins because they make holes in my pockets; and I hate bank notes because, except when they're new, they look dirty and tatty.

b  Do you ever do something for luck, or avoid doing something because doing it may bring you bad luck?

c  What keeps you awake at night?

d  Some people like to sit around watching TV, or sunbathe on the beach. Not me!

e  I remember the main street before they closed it to traffic.

f  I'll never forget looking at my timetable and wondering what exactly the letters CDT stood for.

g  Imagine the scene: the sea is deep blue, trees are swaying in the warm breeze, and you're a day's car journey away from the nearest city.

h  Everyone wants to look their best, but if that means having sore feet and cold hands, I'm not sure that I care that much about my appearance.

## Listening Part 3

1 🔊 1.4 **You will hear five short extracts in which women are talking about their relationships with their brothers. For questions 1–5, choose from the list (A–H) what each speaker says. Use the letters only once. There are three extra letters which you do not need to use.**

ONLY ONE CARD TO GO!

A Her brother had more freedom than she did.

B She never sees him because he's studying away from home.

C Her parents preferred her to her brother.

D She became good friends with her brother in her teens.

E She doesn't keep in touch with her brother because he lives abroad.

F She doesn't make the effort to see her brother nowadays.

G She used to like her brother but doesn't now.

H When she was younger, she was proud of having an older brother.

| | |
|---|---|
| Speaker 1 | **1** ☐ |
| Speaker 2 | **2** ☐ |
| Speaker 3 | **3** ☐ |
| Speaker 4 | **4** ☐ |
| Speaker 5 | **5** ☐ |

## Vocabulary

➕ **Phrasal verbs with *pick***

1 **Replace the words in *italics* in these sentences with the correct form of *pick* and one of these words. You need to use one of the words three times.**

at   on   out   up

a Our plane landed at 4 a.m., so my brother *came to collect us* in his car.

b He's such a bully – he always *treats* younger or weaker people *unfairly*.

c I've got a terrible cold. I probably *caught it* at the swimming pool.

d You can tell when she's worried – she just *eats little bits of* her food.

e She's easy to *spot* in a crowd – she's very tall, and she's got long black hair.

f I *learned* French when I lived in Paris.

***have* and *take***

2 **Complete these sentences with the correct form of *have* or *take*.**

a Do you know what time the ceremony _____ place this afternoon?

b We don't want to _____ children until we're in our late twenties.

c Maria is thinking of _____ a nursing course next year.

d Their children are old enough to _____ care of themselves.

e I don't want to _____ an argument about this. We need to decide.

f I'd like to visit the gallery, but unfortunately we _____ enough time.

# Grammar

## The future

**1 What would you say in these situations? Choose the correct answer.**

a You intend to learn to drive next year.

*I'm going to learn / I'll learn* to drive next year.

b You have arranged to meet your sister this evening.

*I meet / I'm meeting* my sister this evening.

c This time tomorrow, you expect to be in the process of walking to school.

This time tomorrow, *I'll walk / I'll be walking* to school.

d It has become very cold and the sky has turned black. This means snow very soon.

*It's snowing / It's going to snow* very soon.

e You've looked at the train timetable for the weekend. It says the departure time of your train is 7.15 in the morning.

My train *will leave / leaves* at 7.15 in the morning.

f After your exams, your plan is to travel round Europe on a motorbike.

After my exams, *I'm travelling / I'm going to travel* round Europe on a motorbike.

g You've just realized that you have no coffee left. You offer to go and get some.

*I go / I'll go* and get some more.

h You moved into your apartment nearly a year ago. Next Saturday is the anniversary of your move.

On Saturday, *I'll have been living / I'll be living* here for exactly a year.

i There is a strong possibility of a rise in the price of petrol next year. This is your prediction.

I think the price of petrol *will go up / is going up* next year.

j Your plane is scheduled to land at 11.15 at night.

My plane *lands / is going to land* at quarter past eleven.

**2 Some of these sentences use the correct future form, but most of them need correcting. Rewrite them where necessary. The first one is done as an example.**

a We'll have a party on June 16th. It's all arranged.

*We're having a party on June 16th. It's all arranged.*

b I'm giving up smoking if it's the last thing I do!

_____

c The phone's ringing. I'm answering it.

_____

d It's a brilliant film. I'm sure you'll enjoy it.

_____

e Unless they arrive soon, we finish all the food by the time they get here.

_____

f Hurry up – your favourite programme starts in five minutes.

_____

g I expect someone is objecting if you wear jeans to work.

_____

h What do you do when you leave school? Have you got any plans?

_____

**3 Complete these sentences with the correct future form of the verb in brackets.**

a My father _____ (be) eighty years old on his next birthday.

b I feel terrible – I think I _____ (faint).

c I won't be at work tomorrow – I _____ (go) for an interview for a new job.

d We'd better hurry up – the bus _____ (leave) in ten minutes.

e This time tomorrow, you _____ (work) in this office for ten years.

f 'The music's terribly loud.'

'Sorry, I _____ (turn) it down.'

g Next year, I _____ (give up) eating meat – that's definite.

h I hope the exam goes well. We _____ (think) of you all the time during the exam.

# Reading and Use of English Part 5

1 You are going to read an article about a computer scientist. For questions 1–6, choose the answer (A, B, C or D) which you think fits best according to the text.

1 How is Wendy Hall different from many other computer scientists?

A She is fascinated by the technical details of computing.

B She is not as creative as the majority of her colleagues.

C She is not interested in talking about the technicalities of computers.

D She is less well qualified than many of her colleagues.

2 Why was Wendy Hall first attracted to computer science?

A She was interested in computer programming.

B She saw the future potential for the use of computers.

C She became addicted to playing computer games.

D She enjoyed using her own personal computer.

3 What was the purpose of the first software designed by Wendy Hall?

A It helped upload texts on to computers.

B It made information available electronically.

C It enabled teachers to produce educational videos.

D It helped other teachers she worked with.

4 What were Wendy Hall's feelings when she first became a university lecturer?

A She felt out of place as a woman in a man's world.

B She couldn't use the same specialist language as her colleagues.

C She didn't know the answers to questions she was asked.

D She was worried because her colleagues were better qualified than her.

5 How did other researchers react to what Hall proposed?

A They considered her ideas to be an important breakthrough.

B They suggested improvements to her basic ideas.

C They didn't understand the importance of her ideas.

D They said her ideas were not important for computer science in general.

6 How was Tim Berners-Lee's system different from Hall's?

A His system depended on access to the internet.

B His system applied only to individual computers.

C His system could not be used on individual computers.

D His system did not require a computer hard drive.

# It's a Woman's

1 Although Wendy Hall is an internationally-renowned computer scientist, there is nothing geeky about her. In fact, this gregarious woman with a warm laugh is among the best and brightest. As well as heading the University of Southampton's
5 Electronics and Computer Science department, Hall works closely with Tim Berners-Lee, the 'father of the Web'. So why did a woman who is indifferent to writing computer code or discussing processor speed choose a career in IT, a field with a reputation for being dominated by geeky men?

10 Hall's work with computers began in the early 1980s, long before the Web existed and when personal computers were a novelty. 'All you could do with PCs in those days was learn programming or play games,' she says. Like many women at that time, Hall avoided such activities: she was more interested
15 in pure mathematics. Her ability to appreciate abstract ideas is what then drew her to explore the growing field of computer science. She taught herself to program, but it was the thought of how computing could change people's lives that fascinated her. 'I could see what was possible,' she says.

# World Wide Web

20 The primitive graphics on her early computer started her thinking about future possibilities for education. She built simple software to help her colleagues teach at the college where she worked, but her imagination was running wild: 'I was interested in getting text documents and videos onto 25 computers in large quantities. I thought: "Wouldn't it be amazing if all this was available electronically?"'

In 1984 she became a university lecturer specializing in computer science. At first, working among computer scientists was intimidating. 'I always felt inadequate because 30 I didn't talk technical,' she says. 'Questions like "How fast does it go?" or "How much storage does it have?" don't interest me.' Soon, however, it was her powerful imagination and her lack of interest in detail which proved to be her asset.

One of Hall's first ideas was a database of electronic photos, 35 documents and audio recordings that could be linked together in different ways depending on who was using them. 'I wanted different people to be able to ask different questions about a document,' she says. 'For example, a schoolchild would ask different questions from a professor.' 40 Many researchers dismissed her ideas, claiming they were irrelevant to mainstream computer science. But Hall persisted and in 1989 launched Microcosm, a downloadable system that created links between the contents of a document and related information on the hard drive while the user read 45 that document. As she had hoped, her system meant that a schoolchild could be shown different links from a professor looking at the same document.

Coincidentally, 1989 was also the year that Tim Berners-Lee first proposed the World Wide Web. As it turns out it was 50 Berners-Lee's vision, which used links that were embedded within a document, that took off. The World Wide Web worked on a global network, allowing anyone with an internet connection to access it, whereas Wendy Hall's Microcosm only worked in stand-alone hard drives.

55 Does Wendy Hall ever regret leaving pure mathematics and choosing the world of computers? 'Not at all,' she says. 'All the wonderful things I am doing are because I am a computer scientist. IT and computing are the basis of everything.'

## Grammar

*too* and *enough*

> *too* = more than is necessary, allowed or good.
> *This coffee is too hot for me to drink.*
> *It's just a student party – there's no need to dress too formally.*
>
> *enough* = sufficient
> *They're old enough to get married.*
> *The lecturer talked loudly enough for us to hear her.*

1 **Read the information in the box. Then complete sentences a–d with *too* or *enough*.**

   a When I was sixteen, I fell in love with a boy of eighteen. We wanted to get married, but my parents said 'no'. My parents thought we were _____ young and not serious _____ .

   b There's a fantastic apartment right in the town centre, but we can't afford it. The rent is _____ high.

   c I was thinking of going to India for my holiday next year, but I don't think I could stand the high temperatures. I think it would be _____ hot for me.

   d My brother gave up the idea of becoming a teacher because he realized he wasn't patient _____ for the job.

2 **Rewrite these sentences, using the word in brackets. The first one is done as an example.**

   a It's too cold to swim in the sea. (enough)
   *It isn't warm enough to swim in the sea.*

   b You're too young to learn to drive. (enough)
   _____

   c You aren't walking fast enough to keep up with me. (too)
   _____

   d These new jeans are too small for me. (enough)
   _____

   e My brother doesn't live close enough to come for the weekend. (too)
   _____

   f I'm not tall enough to reach the top shelf. (too)
   _____

   g I'm too ill to come on holiday with you. (enough)
   _____

# Reading and Use of English Part 4

1 For questions 1–6, complete the second sentence so that it has a similar meaning to the first sentence, using the word given. Do not change the word given. You must use between two and five words, including the word given. Here is an example (0).

EXAMPLE

0 Jason adds up figures well for someone his age.

**GOOD**

Jason ___*is good at adding up*___ figures for someone his age.

1 We were in too much of a hurry to eat before we left.

**TIME**

We _____ to eat before we left.

2 It is certain that she will pass her music exam.

**BOUND**

She _____ her music exam.

3 I am meeting my tutor at 2 o'clock this afternoon.

**ARRANGED**

I _____ with my tutor at 2 o'clock this afternoon.

4 Many countries have introduced a new law to ban smoking in public places.

**BROUGHT**

In many countries, a new law _____ to ban smoking in public places.

5 It's improbable that we'll ever go there again.

**UNLIKELY**

We _____ there again.

6 Dan learned Russian when he lived with a family in Moscow. He didn't study it formally.

**PICK**

Dan didn't study Russian formally. He _____ living with a family in Moscow.

# Vocabulary

**Personality adjectives**

1 Match the following adjectives with their definitions. An example is given.

| brave caring cheerful creative energetic enthusiastic fair fit hard-working organized patient sociable well-educated |
| --- |

A person who...

a has had a good education.                    ___*well-educated*___

b is always lively and doesn't tire easily.     _____

c is original, artistic and imaginative.         _____

d is calm and does not get annoyed or frustrated.  _____

e is helpful and sympathetic to other people.   _____

f is not afraid of dangerous situations.         _____

g is friendly and enjoys being with other people. _____

h treats everyone equally.                        _____

i is efficient and good at making and carrying out plans. _____

j is healthy and in good physical condition.     _____

k is interested in and excited about something.  _____

l is the opposite of lazy.                        _____

m is always happy and optimistic.                 _____

# Writing Part 1

1 Read paragraphs 1–4, which are taken from a sample answer to the question 'Is it better to work for yourself or for an employer?' Choose the correct topic sentence (a–f) to complete each paragraph. You do not need to use two of the sentences.

a Unfortunately, there are disadvantages to both employment situations.

b Currently, most people who have jobs work for an employer.

c For many people, being self-employed would be too risky.

d To sum up, my own opinion is that there is no clear answer to this question.

e Many people I know have started very successful businesses of their own.

f However, an increasing number of people are now choosing to work for themselves.

1 _____ If they have a good employer, workers are paid regularly and have working conditions of a high standard. This usually means that they have acceptable working hours and paid holidays.

2 _____ This may mean they are starting their own business or working on a freelance basis for more than one client. Many people who are self-employed find this situation gives them more freedom and flexibility to decide when they work.

3 _____ If you work for an employer, you may lose your job or your working conditions may get worse. As for people who work for themselves, they cannot be sure of getting regular wages, or they may have to work very long hours to make a living.

4 _____ There are advantages and disadvantages of working for an employer and working for yourself.

2 Choose the supporting sentence 1–6 which follows each of the topic sentences (a–f) in the way given in brackets.

a It is a fact that people are living longer than they did in the past. (Explanation)

b People's diets have improved in many ways. (Example)

c Some governments are raising the retirement age. (Reason)

d In some cultures, eldest sons are responsible for looking after their elderly parents. (Additional information)

e Many people do not save much money for their retirement. (Result)

f The elderly are treated with great respect in some societies. (Opinion)

1 For instance, people are eating more fruit and vegetables.

2 In my view this is something that old people deserve.

3 They also have to provide for their wives and children.

4 This is due largely to the successful fight against diseases.

5 This is mainly to reduce spending on pensions as people are living longer than in the past.

6 This means that their standard of living falls when they stop working.

# Travel and culture

## Vocabulary

**➕ Travel**

**1 Complete these sentences with the appropriate word from this list.**

| crossing | cruise | excursion | journey | tour | trip | voyage |

a If you live in the south of England, it's easy to go on a day _____ to France.

b Have you ever been on a guided _____ of Westminster Abbey?

c Do you know, my _____ to work took over an hour this morning.

d The price of the holiday includes a full-day _____ to a place of cultural interest.

e The ferry _____ was cancelled because of rough seas.

f Last year, we went on a _____ around the Mediterranean. The ship was very luxurious.

g The Titanic sank on its first transatlantic _____ to New York.

**2 Choose the correct alternative in *italics* in these sentences.**

a We *made / did* a lot of sightseeing when we were in Athens.

b The *campsite / camping* was very crowded, so we had to *install / put up* our tent close to the exit.

c The plane *set down / landed* on time.

d Once the passengers had *got in / boarded* the plane, the cabin *staff / crew* asked them to *fasten / close* their seat belts.

e Next year, we're going on a cheap *package / charter* holiday to Portugal.

f If you *lose / miss* the train, you'll just have to wait for the next one.

g The *bus / coach* trip to Bruges was fully *booked / reserved*.

h On the cruise, when we stopped at the major *ports / harbours*, most of the passengers *got out / disembarked*.

i Did you *make / take* a lot of photos while you were away?

j It's much more interesting to drive on country *ways / lanes* than motorways.

k She bought the hand-carved elephant as a *souvenir / memory* of her safari holiday.

**Phrasal verbs: travel**  **3** Complete these sentences with an appropriate phrasal verb from this list in an appropriate form.

| check in | drop off | pick up | see off | set off | stop over | take off |

a My flight is arriving in the early morning. Could you come and _____ me _____ ?

b They _____ for the airport at 8 a.m., so they should be there by now.

c As soon as we arrived at the airport, we _____ and went through to the departure lounge.

d When Richard left for university, his family and friends went to the station to _____ him _____ .

e The flight was delayed, and the plane _____ three hours late.

f We're going to _____ in Hong Kong for a couple of days on our way to New Zealand.

g I'll _____ you _____ at the terminal before I park the car.

➕ **Expressions with *spare***  **4** Complete these sentences with the appropriate word from this list.

| change | parts | room | seat | time | tyre |

a Last year, I went to France on a day trip with some friends. They were taking their car and asked if I wanted to come as they had a spare _____ .

b You should carry a spare _____ in case you get a puncture.

c We can easily put you up when you come. You can sleep in the spare _____ .

d Apart from going out with friends, what do you like doing in your spare _____ ?

e It's difficult to get spare _____ for old cars when they break down.

f I wasn't able to give the beggar any money as I didn't have any spare _____ on me.

# Listening Part 3

1 🔊 1.5 You will hear five short extracts in which people are talking about journeys they have been on. For questions 1–5, choose from the list (A–H) what each speaker says. Use the letters only once. There are three extra letters which you do not need to use.

A The journey took much longer than expected.

B The staff were very helpful.

C I found this way of travelling uncomfortable.

D I was exhausted by the end of the trip.

E I was slightly disappointed by the experience.

F I would travel this way again.

G I met some interesting people travelling.

H Travelling this way was an adventure.

| Speaker 1 | **1** | |
| Speaker 2 | **2** | |
| Speaker 3 | **3** | |
| Speaker 4 | **4** | |
| Speaker 5 | **5** | |

# Grammar

## Past tenses

**1** Choose the correct alternative in *italics* in these sentences.

a Jan *was going / went* to live in Italy in 2010. She hadn't been in the country long before she *got / was getting* married.

b '*Didn't you finish / Haven't you finished* your homework yet, Alex? You *have been doing / have done* it for ages.'
'I *did / have done* most of it, but I'm stuck on the last bit.'

c I know I said I'd phone you as soon as I *got / had got* back but I can't remember where I *have been writing down / wrote down* your new number.

d It's typical, isn't it? I *had just put / just put* shampoo on my hair when the phone *had rung / rang*. I *was thinking / thought* it might be important, so I *have rushed / rushed* downstairs. Needless to say, it *had stopped / has stopped* ringing before I *was reaching / reached* it.

e 'I'm terribly sorry, but I *have forgotten / forgot* your name.'

f Police said that the man they wanted to question *had / was having* long hair and *has been wearing / was wearing* a denim jacket and jeans. He *was driving off / had driven off* in a stolen car.

g Julie *has just covered / had just covered* herself in suntan lotion when the sun *went / had gone* behind a large black cloud.

h I *was thinking / have thought* of calling Sam and *have just picked up / had just picked up* my address book to look up her number when the phone *started / was starting* ringing. It was her!

i 'Is anything the matter?'
'No. I *have peeled / have been peeling* onions. Onions always make me cry.'

j I *was sitting / sat* on the bus on my way to work when I realized I *left / had left* something cooking on the stove.

**2** Complete this story with verbs from the list below. Use an appropriate past tense and make any other changes that are necessary.

| ask | get in | leave | pick up | see |
|-----|--------|-------|---------|-----|
| begin | get out | make | rain | shake |
| drive | give | notice | reach | try |
| drive off | have | open | realize | wait |

# The Mysterious Hitchhiker

One evening, a young woman **(1)** _____ through lonely countryside. It **(2)** _____ heavily and it **(3)** _____ to get dark. Suddenly, she **(4)** _____ an old woman by the side of the road, holding her thumb out as if she wanted a lift. 'I can't leave her out in this weather,' the young woman said to herself. So she stopped the car and **(5)** _____ the door. 'Do you want a lift?' she **(6)** _____ . The old woman nodded and **(7)** _____ .

As she **(8)** _____ herself comfortable, the young woman asked her, '**(9)** _____ you _____ long?'

The old woman **(10)** _____ her head. 'You were lucky, then,' the young woman commented, wondering why the old woman never spoke. She **(11)** _____ again. 'Nasty weather for the time of year,' she continued. The old woman nodded in agreement. No matter what the young woman said, the hitchhiker **(12)** _____ no answer except for a nod or a shake of the head.

All of a sudden, the young woman **(13)** _____ that her passenger's hands were very large and hairy. With a shock she **(14)** _____ that the hitchhiker wasn't an old woman at all but a man dressed up as an old woman. She braked suddenly. 'I can't see out of the rear window,' she explained. 'Would you mind cleaning it for me?' The hitchhiker nodded and opened the car door. As soon as the hitchhiker **(15)** _____ of the car, the terrified woman **(16)** _____ at top speed.

When she **(17)** _____ the next village, she stopped. She noticed that the hitchhiker **(18)** _____ a handbag behind. She **(19)** _____ it _____ and opened it. Inside the bag was a gun. She **(20)** _____ a narrow escape!

# Reading and Use of English Part 1

**1** For questions 1–8, read the text below and decide which answer (A, B, C or D) best fits each gap. There is an example at the beginning (0).

# Near-misses

As the skies around the world's airports get more and more **(0)** __C__ , the number of potentially dangerous incidents is **(1)** _____ .

Officials are **(2)** _____ studying a recent incident where a jumbo jet flew so low over nearby houses that everyone thought a crash was **(3)** _____ . One of the plane's four engines had failed just after take-off. The pilot put the other engines on full speed to **(4)** _____ him to get high enough to drop most of the plane's fuel. His calmness and experience helped him to **(5)** _____ what could have been a terrible disaster. Somewhat surprisingly, however, it was a further thirty minutes before the pilot received **(6)** _____ to land due to other incoming flights.

Although this sort of incident is becoming more and more **(7)** _____ , it still remains a / an **(8)** _____ that it is safer to fly than to cross the road.

| | | | | |
|---|---|---|---|---|
| **0** | **A** packed | **B** full | **C** crowded | **D** filled |
| **1** | **A** spreading | **B** raising | **C** developing | **D** increasing |
| **2** | **A** momentarily | **B** currently | **C** nowadays | **D** actually |
| **3** | **A** definite | **B** certain | **C** inevitable | **D** sure |
| **4** | **A** let | **B** manage | **C** enable | **D** make |
| **5** | **A** escape | **B** pass | **C** miss | **D** avoid |
| **6** | **A** permission | **B** permit | **C** allowance | **D** approval |
| **7** | **A** common | **B** normal | **C** ordinary | **D** general |
| **8** | **A** proof | **B** fact | **C** evidence | **D** truth |

# Reading and Use of English Part 6

1 You are going to read a newspaper article about a future expedition to the planet Mars. Six sentences have been removed from the article. Choose from the sentences A–G the one which fits each gap (1–6). There is one extra sentence which you do not need to use.

A They are looking for applicants who are healthy, smart enough to learn new skills and able to function in a small group.

B The viewing figures and income they brought in were also influential.

C One would have to agree with their reaction, given that the privately-financed plan does not involve a return journey.

D Applications had been expected to be around the one million mark, however.

E The pioneers will also face lethal hazards such as high doses of cosmic radiation and potentially toxic Martian dust.

F This is the number of people who have so far offered to join an ambitious private mission to send a group of four men and women to Mars in 2023.

G And the final total could rise even higher before the deadline for applications is reached.

# One-way ticket to Mars

1 A one-way ticket to another planet where there is no air, no water or food – and certainly no return home – may not sound like a lot of fun. However, to the 165,000 applicants, the opportunity to live permanently on Mars has been too tempting
5 to ignore. **1** They will be the first intrepid pioneers for a permanent space colony on the Red Planet.

The organizers of the Mars One mission said they were surprised by how many people had offered to become the first astronauts to land and live on Mars. **2** This is not because it would be
10 impossible, but because of the technical difficulty and cost of fuelling the trip home.

Each applicant has had to pay on average $25, depending on their country, to cover the administrative fees of the selection process. Nevertheless, even this small financial penalty has
15 failed to dissuade the tens of thousands who dream of going to Mars. **3** The quality of the applicants is very high, according to Bas Lansdorp, the Dutch entrepreneur who dreamed up the scheme last year.

Lansdorp's plan is to create a media event which is 'exciting,
20 inspiring and beautiful', just like the Olympic Games, which gave him his idea. **4** The estimated £4bn cost of the Mars mission will be met by television rights and other kinds of media sponsorship, and although Big Brother creator, Paul Romer, is one of those sitting on the Mars One board, the event
25 will not be a TV reality show.

A selection committee will begin to sort the applicants in the coming weeks, and shortlists will be drawn up in the coming year. **5** Nearly a quarter of the applicants live in the United States. The space nations of China, Brazil, India and Russia
30 come next on the list of the 140 countries where the applicants live. Britain comes in 6th place with about 7,000. The plan is to build teams of four people, each from a different continent, who will live and train together for seven years before the first manned launch in 2022, arriving the following year.

35 Rockets carrying cargo, food and living modules will be sent to Mars a few years in advance of the manned landing. A further crew of four people will arrive two years after the first astronauts have landed. Lansdorp insisted that the mission was viable, even though drinking water will have to be collected
40 from the Martian soil by robotic explorers before the astronauts are able to land. **6**

But perhaps the biggest obstacle of all will be the psychological anxiety of knowing there is no return journey no matter what happens. 'They will only step into the rocket if they really want
45 to go. The risk is theirs and they can't change their mind once they are on the way,' Mr Lansdorp said.

# Vocabulary

**Extreme adjectives**

**1** Find the extreme adjectives which correspond to these normal adjectives. The words can go in any direction.

| angry | big | cold | dirty | funny | hot | small | tasty | tired |

| F | N | E | C | D | E | T | J | I | H | O | P | S | A |
|---|---|---|---|---|---|---|---|---|---|---|---|---|---|
| R | A | X | U | E | P | V | Q | M | F | U | U | E | D |
| E | I | H | I | L | A | R | I | O | U | S | G | G | F |
| E | F | A | B | I | D | R | U | N | R | I | L | E | F |
| Z | G | U | T | C | B | O | I | L | I | N | G | W | I |
| I | K | S | B | I | C | X | Z | F | O | H | I | P | L |
| N | L | T | P | O | I | Y | R | D | U | A | D | T | T |
| G | J | E | P | U | K | N | E | T | S | U | I | O | H |
| S | E | D | I | S | T | S | B | M | T | I | N | Y | Y |

**Negative adjectives**

**2** Write the missing nouns and the negative forms of these adjectives. An example is given.

| Adjective | Noun | Negative adjective |
|---|---|---|
| **a** moral | _morality_ | _immoral_ |
| **b** successful | _____ | _____ |
| **c** honest | _____ | _____ |
| **d** mature | _____ | _____ |
| **e** patient | _____ | _____ |
| **f** responsible | _____ | _____ |

# Writing Part 2

**Creating interest**

**1** The adjectives *nice*, *good* and *bad* are often over used. They can be replaced by other adjectives which make a description more vivid. Replace the adjectives in *italics* with the most appropriate adjective from this list. Use each adjective only once.

| accomplished | delicious | disastrous | enjoyable | kind | naughty |
| pretty | serious | sunny | useful | well-behaved |

**a** The holiday was *good*. The food in the hotel was very good, and we had *good* weather every day.

**b** The family we stayed with were very *nice*. They made us a *nice* picnic to take with us the day we left.

**c** It was a *very bad* holiday. Everything went wrong. On the way there, we were involved in a *bad* accident, but amazingly no one was hurt.

**d** At the festival all the women wore *nice* dresses in many different patterns.

**e** My brother Jacob, who took part in the parade, plays the trumpet. He is a very *good* musician.

**f** Holiday companies usually give *good* advice about what you should and shouldn't do when you travel abroad.

**g** 6 January is when most Spanish children get their presents. Children are warned that they will only get a present if they are *good*. If they are *bad*, they will just get a piece of coal.

## Reading and Use of English Part 6

1 You are going to read an article about sleepwalking. Six sentences have been removed from the article. Choose from the sentences A–G the one which fits each gap (1–6). There is one extra sentence which you do not need to use.

A It turned out that she had been making them in her sleep.

B She did not realize that anything was wrong at first.

C These work by temporarily stopping the body entering the phase of sleep which accompanies sleepwalking.

D She does not look forward to turning the lights out at night.

E It may seem amazing, but all these kinds of things are possible.

F Others include severe tiredness or the excessive consumption of alcohol.

G In the majority of cases, the experience is quite uneventful.

# Walk on the Dark Side

## *Mike Thomson reports on a disturbing phenomenon: sleepwalking.*

1 Dangerous as well as embarrassing, sleepwalking remains a mystery, while its results can be both upsetting and unpredictable. Despite their popular image as zombie-like figures who stumble about with outstretched arms,
5 sleepwalkers are often capable of performing complex acts. Dr Peter Fenick says their capabilities are surprising. 'I've known sleepwalkers who have got onto motorbikes, ridden horses, and driven cars.' 1☐

Some sleep disorder experts believe that such complex
10 behaviour occurs when the individual is suffering from nocturnal blackouts or amnesia. These produce what is called the 'fugue' state. In this condition, the individual enters a lighter state of sleep and can cope more easily with lengthier and more complicated tasks than the average sleepwalker,
15 who is usually back in bed within fifteen minutes.

Whatever the definition given, however, few people are as clear-thinking and articulate when they are asleep as Janet Brierly from London, who found that her phone bill had mysteriously trebled. She later discovered why. Friends
20 would remark on lengthy late-night calls she had made to them (many of them international), none of which she remembered. 2☐ She has since been forced to hide her telephone in a drawer at night.

It is estimated that as many as one in three children and one
25 in twenty adults sleepwalk at some time. Experts believe the condition is most common among children and the elderly, though the reason for this remains a mystery. What is now becoming clear is that sleepwalking tends to run in families. Stress or anxiety are believed to be major causes. 3☐

30 Sleepwalking is thought to start about ninety minutes after a person goes to sleep. 4☐ It leads to little more than a walk round the bedroom or the opening of a few drawers. Injuries most often occur when sleepwalkers believe they are somewhere they are not: windows, stairs and electrical
35 appliances can lead to disaster.

Nancy Harrison from Wiltshire woke up shivering one night to find the bedroom window wide open and her husband Robert's bed empty. 5☐ 'I assumed Robert had gone to the bathroom. But when I went to close the window, I saw his

# Vocabulary

➕ **Word building**

1 Complete the table with the nouns related to the adjectives given.

| Noun | Adjective | Noun | Adjective |
|------|-----------|------|-----------|
|  | embarrassed |  | disappointed |
|  | bored |  | amused |
|  | annoyed |  | frustrated |
|  | exhausted |  | surprised |

➕ **-ed and -ing adjectives**

2 Read the information in the box below. Then choose the correct alternative in *italics* in sentences a–j.

> *-ed* adjectives describe the way someone looks or feels.
> *John is bored. He wants a change.*
>
> *-ing* adjectives describe the effect someone or something has on other people.
> *John is boring. No one wants to sit next to him.*

a Sleepwalking can be dangerous as well as *embarrassed / embarrassing*.

b Working in an office can be so *bored / boring*. You do the same things every day.

c I got so *annoyed / annoying* with the man that I ended up shouting at him.

d I was so *embarrassed / embarrassing* when I went to pay the bill and realized I didn't have enough money. I went bright red!

e Pete was extremely *frustrated / frustrating* when he couldn't find the last answer to the crossword.

f The trip was great but *exhausted / exhausting*. I need a holiday to recover!

g I didn't find the joke particularly *amused / amusing*, but I laughed anyway.

h Try not to be too *disappointed / disappointing*. Most people don't pass their driving test first time.

i It was so *embarrassed / embarrassing* when I couldn't remember her name. I didn't know where to look.

j I think I'll just go to bed. I'm absolutely *exhausted / exhausting*.

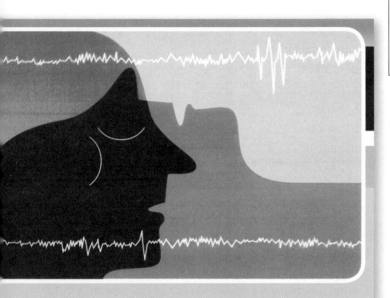

40 body lying on the lawn. I was really scared. I couldn't believe he could still be alive, and I dashed downstairs. But when I bent down to check if he was still breathing, I discovered he was unhurt and still asleep.' In another instance, a Birmingham woman poured hot water over herself while she
45 was sleepwalking. When she woke up five hours later, she was covered in red marks.

Trying to find the root cause of the problem of why people sleepwalk is not straightforward. There are several sleep laboratories and clinics around the country, but most
50 concentrate on treating more common complaints such as snoring or insomnia. To see a specialist, you need to be referred by your own doctor, who may first try you on sleeping pills. **6** ☐ Their addictive nature, however, means they can only be a short-term solution.

# Grammar

## Gerunds and infinitives

**1** Complete these sentences with an appropriate preposition and verb in the gerund form from the lists below. You can use the prepositions more than once. An example is given.

| against | of | become | do | pass |
| at | on | bring | draw | persuade |
| for | with | break | get | put up |
| in | | come | leave | speak |

**a** I do apologize _for bringing_ Rachel to your party, but she insisted _____ .

**b** Most politicians are extremely skilled _____ in public.

**c** Even though he was bored _____ the same thing day in day out, he never made an effort to look for a new job.

**d** A good salesperson is clever _____ people to buy things they don't really need.

**e** I'm not responsible _____ the vase. It was Greg's fault.

**f** Due to the increasing number of burglaries in the area, the police are warning people _____ their windows open.

**g** Jack is quite capable _____ good marks at school, but he never does.

**h** The examiner congratulated Graeme _____ his driving test first time.

**i** Despite the strong wind, we succeeded _____ our tent.

**j** David is good _____ , but he isn't really interested _____ an architect.

**2** Complete these sentences with the gerund or infinitive form of the verbs in brackets. Remember that some verbs can take both the infinitive and the gerund but with a change of meaning.

**a** If you don't stop _____ (waste) time and at least try _____ (get) the report finished today, the boss will be furious.

**b** 'We regret _____ (inform) passengers of the cancellation of the 10.06 train to Glasgow.'

**c** The directions she gave me were easy _____ (follow), so I was amazed _____ (find) I still got lost.

**d** I meant _____ (get up) earlier, but I forgot _____ (set) my alarm clock.

**e** My uncle didn't give up _____ (smoke), even after the doctor told him he risked _____ (have) a heart attack.

**f** Pleased _____ (meet) you. Glad _____ (hear) you're enjoying your stay.

**g** Can you imagine _____ (be) famous and _____ (have) enough money to do whatever you wanted?

**h** Have you considered _____ (get) a part-time job to make some extra money?

# Vocabulary

## Personal qualities

**1** Which of the adjectives below describe positive personal qualities (P), which describe negative personal qualities (N), and which could be either positive or negative (P / N)?

**a** boring _____

**b** optimistic _____

**c** determined _____

**d** *efficient* _____

**e** *friendly* _____

**f** *patient* _____

**g** sensible _____

**h** serious _____

**i** *emotional* _____

**j** jealous _____

**k** envious _____

**l** thoughtful _____

**2** What prefixes are added to the adjectives in *italics* in **1** to make them negative?

**3** What are the nouns related to each of the adjectives in **1**?

Streeter

**4 Complete these sentences with an appropriate adjective or noun.**

a Harry is a 'glass half full' kind of person. He's _____ and always looks on the bright side.

b _____ , also known as 'the green-eyed monster', is often the result of insecurity.

c Anna is a very _____ girl. You can trust her not to do anything foolhardy.

d It was _____ of you to invite Lisa's ex-boyfriend and his new girlfriend to the party. You know she's still in love with him.

e I thought the meeting would never end. I almost died of _____ .

f _____ is an important attribute of success. If you really want something, you have to keep trying.

g Scottish people are well known for their _____ . They will readily talk to strangers.

h There's no point being _____ when you are in a queue. You won't get to the front any quicker!

# Reading and Use of English Part 4

1 For questions 1–6, complete the second sentence so that it has a similar meaning to the first sentence, using the word given. Do not change the word given. You must use between two and five words, including the word given. Here is an example (0).

EXAMPLE

0 Jason adds up figures well for someone his age.

**GOOD**

Jason ___*is good at adding up*___ figures for someone his age.

1 I couldn't hear what he said because of the noise.

**PREVENTED**

The noise _____ what he said.

2 Jane continued to work for the firm after the baby was born.

**WENT**

Jane _____ for the firm after the baby was born.

3 She had no intention of insulting you.

**MEAN**

She _____ you.

4 I have no objection to Paul coming as well.

**MIND**

I do _____ as well.

5 Predicting the weather is sometimes difficult.

**HARD**

It can _____ the weather.

6 It's getting easier for me to get up early.

**USED**

I _____ up early.

# Vocabulary

**Collocations**

**1** **Complete these sentences with an appropriate adjective from this list. One adjective is used more than once.**

| close | hard | heavy | serious | strong |
|---|---|---|---|---|

**a** Unemployment is a _____ problem nowadays.

**b** The forecast for tomorrow is for _____ winds and rain in the west, and scattered showers elsewhere.

**c** He said he had been held up in _____ traffic.

**d** I went on holiday with a _____ friend.

**e** Trying to explain how the internet works to people who have never used a computer is _____ work.

**f** The punishment for _____ crimes like murder is life imprisonment.

**2** **Complete these sentences with an adverb or a verb from this list in the appropriate form.**

| attentively | become | express | find | hard (x2) | heavily | passionately |
|---|---|---|---|---|---|---|
| soundly | take | | | | | |

**a** I was sleeping so _____ that I didn't hear my alarm go off.

**b** Governments need to _____ a solution to the problem of global warming.

**c** If you work _____ , you'll be finished by lunchtime.

**d** You can _____ the exam three times a year.

**e** The motorist had been drinking _____ and was well over the limit.

**f** The wet weather is _____ a problem for farmers, who need to harvest their crops soon.

**g** Everyone listened _____ to what the boss was saying.

**h** The politician argued his point _____ and almost convinced me he was right.

**i** I had to think _____ before I remembered where I had seen him before.

**j** She _____ the opinion that there was too much violence on TV.

**3** **Choose the correct alternative in *italics*. Sometimes both words are possible.**

**a** When we were on holiday, we *went on / took* a *short / small* coach trip to Loch Ness.

**b** It was a *tough / hard* decision to *make / do*.

**c** She had *spent / passed* her life helping others.

**d** The store has a *wide / big* range of products.

**e** Competition for the contract was *fierce / hard*.

**f** People who *violate / break* the law should be punished.

**g** I can't afford to *run / keep* a car even though I *direct / run* my own business.

**h** There are reports of *important / severe* delays on the Central Line.

**i** The motorist admitted to *breaking / passing* the speed limit.

**j** The bookshelf came with *full / complete* instructions on how to build it.

**k** I'm afraid I wasn't *giving / paying* attention to what she was saying.

**l** We *rented / hired* a car for a few days when we were on holiday.

**m** The band Coldplay will be *playing / performing* live on TV.

**n** The dream was so *clear / vivid* it seemed real.

## Listening Part 2

1 🔊 1.6 You will hear a man called Simon Fuller giving a talk on fish. For questions 1–10, complete the sentences with a word or short phrase.

### The minds of fish

Simon says that some fish are confident, whereas others are [ 1 ] .

Fish have the reputation of only being able to remember things for [ 2 ] .

In one experiment, fish learned that they could escape through the [ 3 ] .

The fish were still able to remember the escape route after [ 4 ] .

Fish have also been trained to tell the difference between types of [ 5 ] .

When the lips of trout were injected with bee venom, they behaved like unhappy [ 6 ] .

Fish appear to reduce pain by [ 7 ] the painful area.

Some scientists believe that creatures that don't have a neocortex are unable to [ 8 ] .

Simon thinks it's better to keep goldfish in [ 9 ] .

Simon says it's important to keep goldfish [ 10 ] if you want them to stay healthy.

## Writing Part 1

1 Read this essay. Divide it into four paragraphs, adding any missing commas, full stops and capital letters.

**Music is the best therapy if you are feeling sad or depressed. Do you agree?**

Music plays an important role in many people's lives. Whether it is classical music pop music rock music jazz or opera, we all listen to it at one time or another for a variety of reasons. Music can certainly affect our mood but the kind of music we listen to will affect our mood differently. Upbeat music generally makes people feel happy while slow music particularly if it reminds us of a painful event in our past can make us feel sad. If we are feeling sad or depressed music may lift our spirits however there are many other activities people can do. Many people find that doing exercise is effective. For other people spending time with friends has the same positive effect on their mood being out in the countryside or by the sea can also work. To sum up music may be a good therapy for some people when they are feeling low, but for others it can have the opposite effect there are many other activities which people can do which are equally, if not more, effective.

## Listening Part 4

1 🔊 1.7 **You will hear part of a radio interview with Jerry, a student who works on a railway. For questions 1–7, choose the best answer (A, B or C).**

1 What was the original purpose of the railway?

   **A** to carry passengers to a large town

   **B** to transport goods to the sea

   **C** to take miners to and from work

2 What is the main use of the railway now?

   **A** It is a place that tourists enjoy visiting.

   **B** It is for villagers to travel to town on.

   **C** It is a centre for educational visits.

3 What kind of work does Jerry do?

   **A** He does a range of different jobs.

   **B** He drives the engines.

   **C** He cleans the engines.

4 Why is repairing engines appropriate work for Jerry?

   **A** He went on trains like this when he was younger.

   **B** He is studying engineering at university.

   **C** He has always found it interesting.

5 When are the engines repaired?

   **A** during the spring and summer

   **B** at weekends

   **C** when not many tourists are there

6 What is the main reason the railway needs money?

   **A** to pay essential employees

   **B** to fund new projects

   **C** to buy coal for the steam trains

7 Why do some adults particularly enjoy their visit?

   **A** They like to see their children happy.

   **B** They find the visitor centre interesting.

   **C** The train journey reminds them of the past.

# Vocabulary

**➕ Expressions with *time***

1 Complete these sentences with the correct form of one of these expressions.

| run out of time | (to) save time | spare time |
| time off | time to kill | waste of time |

a I'm afraid we've _____ . We'll have to arrange another meeting.

b Why don't we both tidy up? That would _____ .

c A holiday this year is out of the question. I don't get any more _____ until next summer.

d Word puzzles are great if you're on a long journey and have _____ .

e I hate doing housework. I think it's a complete _____ .

f If I had more _____ , I'd learn to play a musical instrument.

# Grammar

**Passive or active**

1 Complete these sentences with the word in brackets, using the correct tense of the active or passive form.

a It's a huge company. Two thousand people _____ (employ) there.

b The explosion _____ (happen) just after 9 p.m. Fortunately, no one _____ (hurt).

c The hotel we stayed at was quite good. The rooms _____ (clean) every day and they _____ (change) the towels every other day.

d He only has himself to blame. He _____ (warn) he could lose his licence the next time he _____ (catch) speeding.

e All the children _____ (send) home when the school's central heating system _____ (break down) last winter.

f The watch isn't worth much, but it has sentimental value. It _____ (give) to me on my eighteenth birthday.

g Five hundred employees _____ (make) redundant since the company _____ (take over) six months ago.

h I wonder why Michael _____ (not invite) to Lee's party next Saturday. Everyone else is going.

i Your homework should _____ (hand in) on Friday at the latest.

j We _____ (announce) the winner of our competition at tomorrow's show.

2 Rewrite these passive sentences, changing the passive verbs in *italics* into the active voice. You may have to think of a subject for some of the sentences you write.

a The church *has already been booked*, and the invitations *have been sent out*, so we can't cancel the wedding now.

_____

b Food must not *be brought into* the classroom.

_____

c The dog needs *to be fed* twice a day. Don't forget.

_____

d For a moment, Angie thought she *was being followed* by a strangely-dressed woman.

_____

e In Britain, people's rubbish *is collected* once a week.

_____

**have / get something done**

3 Complete sentences a–j with the correct form of *have / get something done* and one of these verbs.

| check | clean | cut | cut down | decorate | deliver |
| design | repair | take out | test | | |

a The new television is too heavy for me to carry, so I _____ it _____ this afternoon.

b Next week, my parents _____ their bedroom _____ . They've already chosen the paint.

c My camera broke while we were on holiday, so as soon as we got home, I took it back _____ it _____ .

d I spilled coffee all over my best suit, so I _____ it _____ tomorrow.

e A tall tree in the garden was making our house very dark, so we _____ it _____ last week.

f One of my back teeth was very painful, so I went to the dentist's and _____ it _____ .

g My hair's very long, so I'm _____ it _____ this afternoon.

h I think I might need new glasses, so I _____ my eyes _____ tomorrow.

i Do you like our new house? We _____ it _____ by a well-known architect.

j She's been feeling very tired recently, so she went to the doctor's to _____ her blood pressure _____ .

# Reading and Use of English Part 7

1 You are going to read a text on page 43 about cooking. For questions 1–10, choose from the sections (A–D). The sections may be chosen more than once.

**Which person**

| | |
|---|---|
| attempts to copy food they had when they were eating out? | 1 |
| has had experience of cooking pre-prepared food? | 2 |
| is considering having cookery tuition? | 3 |
| is sure they will continue to cook well into the future? | 4 |
| learns to cook new things by trial and error? | 5 |
| learned about cooking when they were abroad? | 6 |
| started cooking to save money? | 7 |
| thinks they have a natural talent for cooking? | 8 |
| was encouraged to cook by one of their parents? | 9 |
| would like to work in a field related to cookery? | 10 |

# Vocabulary

**Dependent prepositions**

1 Complete the phrases in *italics* in these sentences with the correct prepositions. These phrases are used in the reading texts.

a I don't like it when people *ask* _____ *my opinions*.

b I usually *hang out* _____ *my friends* at the weekends.

c In our family, my mother was always *in charge* _____ *making meals*.

d Helen has never been particularly *keen* _____ *cooking*.

e My dad is always *experimenting* _____ *new combinations of spices*.

f My parents think it's a waste to *spend too much money* _____ *food*.

g Many of the world's most famous recipes were *invented* _____ *accident*.

h My friend *learned Russian* _____ *scratch* in less than six months.

i Do you *have any ideas* _____ *suitable dishes*?

➕ **Phrasal verbs with *come***

2 Complete these sentences with the appropriate form of *come* and a word from this list.

| across | out | round (x2) | up | up with |
|---|---|---|---|---|

a I rarely buy hardback books – they're so expensive. I always wait till they _____ in paperback.

b I _____ this while I was cleaning out a cupboard the other day. Is it yours?

c You won't forget that Paula and Nick _____ for dinner on Saturday, will you?

d I can't think what to buy Zoe for her birthday. If you _____ any good ideas, let me know.

e When Jane heard the news, she fainted. When she _____, she didn't know where she was.

f I'm afraid I'll have to cancel the meeting. Something _____ at home.

# Cooking's fun!

**Four enthusiasts talk about why they enjoy cooking.**

## A Jayne Malorey

1 I'm not sure where my passion for cooking comes from. I was probably born with it. But I was also given opportunities to cook when I was young, so that by my early teens I was in charge of making the family meals, and I always loved 5 it. Today, my favourite dishes are from cookery websites or TV shows. I've got a range of good, cheap standbys, like casseroles; but recently, I've started putting stronger flavours into my cooking – I'm really keen on Asian food, especially Indian. I hope to go one day. I learn mainly by 10 experimenting with new tastes. Sometimes they don't work out, but other times they're absolutely delicious. My secret is using simple ingredients in the right combinations. My aim is to learn from the best chefs in the world – I'd really like to go on courses at some of their restaurants.

## B Ed Boden

15 I'm fifteen, but I'm as keen on cooking as any professional chef. It's my only real interest. I'd even rather watch food programmes on TV than hang out with my friends. Whenever I tell anyone, they think it's sweet, but actually it is much more than that. I already know that when I finish 20 my education I want to be a chef. I thought about doing cookery at college, but I've decided against it. Although my dad has a cooking background, I basically taught myself – and I'm a lot more passionate about cooking than he is. What my parents don't understand is that I couldn't live 25 without cooking. They think it's a waste of time and money, but I don't agree. I don't understand how so many people these days just eat ready meals – I love real cooking and I wouldn't give it up for the world.

## C Christina Santos

I don't think cooking is something I'm naturally good at, but 30 I got interested because I needed to spend less on family meals. I started cooking simple meals with inexpensive ingredients, but now I'll cook almost anything – pasta dishes, fish and chicken, curries – I could go on. I also like imitating dishes I've had in restaurants. My roots are in Mexican 35 cookery, and my grandma and mother showed me the basics of that when I was very young; then I learned to cook properly in one of my previous jobs – by accident, really. I was a cook at a restaurant that made everything from fresh ingredients. In places I'd worked at before, cooking meant 40 defrosting food and sticking it in the microwave. Following recipes at work made me want to go home and experiment. Now, my husband and my children are enjoying my cooking talents, but I wouldn't want to do it for a living again.

## D Jean-Paul Montbel

When I was a kid, my father took over the kitchen every 45 Sunday and I helped him. He was a passionate cook and loved to experiment; he made me feel like everything we cooked was exciting. He always asked for my opinions. Now, I enjoy making cakes and biscuits, trying new ideas for salads, as well as making Italian dishes. But what I really enjoy doing 50 is looking in our fridge and cupboards and inventing new recipes from what we've got. My family call these 'emergency recipes' – but they always love the result – and it saves going shopping. My parents taught me my first steps in cooking. Later, I learned a lot from my sister-in-law who is a very good 55 cook. Since I was a child, I've loved collecting recipes, but I've never wanted to cook things I've had out. I lived in Italy for some time and picked up some good tips there.

# Reading and Use of English Part 1

1 For questions 1–8, read the text below and decide which answer (A, B, C or D) best fits each gap. There is an example at the beginning (0).

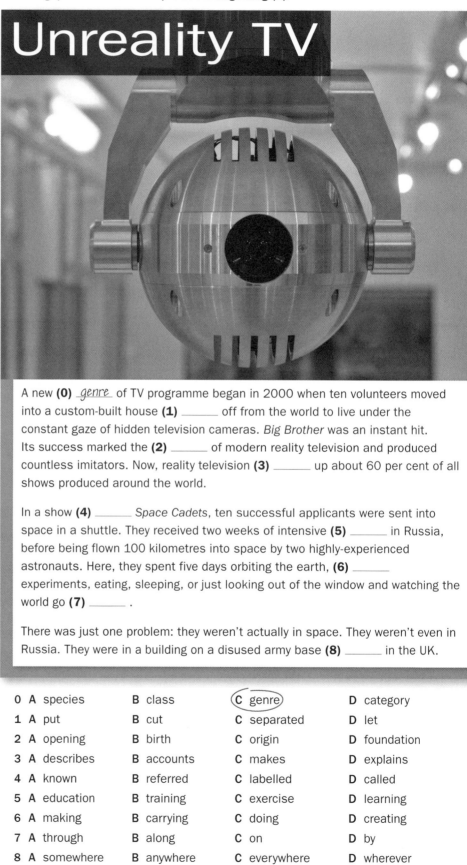

# Unreality TV

A new **(0)** _genre_ of TV programme began in 2000 when ten volunteers moved into a custom-built house **(1)** _____ off from the world to live under the constant gaze of hidden television cameras. *Big Brother* was an instant hit. Its success marked the **(2)** _____ of modern reality television and produced countless imitators. Now, reality television **(3)** _____ up about 60 per cent of all shows produced around the world.

In a show **(4)** _____ *Space Cadets*, ten successful applicants were sent into space in a shuttle. They received two weeks of intensive **(5)** _____ in Russia, before being flown 100 kilometres into space by two highly-experienced astronauts. Here, they spent five days orbiting the earth, **(6)** _____ experiments, eating, sleeping, or just looking out of the window and watching the world go **(7)** _____ .

There was just one problem: they weren't actually in space. They weren't even in Russia. They were in a building on a disused army base **(8)** _____ in the UK.

| 0 | A species | B class | C genre | D category |
|---|-----------|---------|----------|------------|
| 1 | A put | B cut | C separated | D let |
| 2 | A opening | B birth | C origin | D foundation |
| 3 | A describes | B accounts | C makes | D explains |
| 4 | A known | B referred | C labelled | D called |
| 5 | A education | B training | C exercise | D learning |
| 6 | A making | B carrying | C doing | D creating |
| 7 | A through | B along | C on | D by |
| 8 | A somewhere | B anywhere | C everywhere | D wherever |

(0 answer C genre is circled)

# Writing Part 2 – Letter / email

**1** Match a beginning a–f with a suitable ending 1–6. An example is given.

**Beginnings**

a  As regards recent experience,          _5_

b  As far as travelling is concerned,      _____

c  Regarding my salary,                    _____

d  In answer to your second question,      _____

e  As for getting on with colleagues,      _____

f  Moving on to my long-term plans,        _____

**Endings**

**1**  will I be paid on an hourly or a weekly basis?

**2**  I have a reputation for being easy to work with.

**3**  I am used to driving rather than travelling by train.

**4**  I hope to run my own production company eventually.

**5**  my last job was working as a TV cameraman.

**6**  no, I'm not particularly interested in working abroad.

**2** Now rewrite sentences a–e below, adding the focusing expressions in brackets. You may have to change the word order of the first sentence and in some cases add or omit one or more words.

EXAMPLE

*We haven't decided where to go for our next summer holiday yet. (With regard to …)*

*With regard to our next summer holiday, we haven't decided where to go yet.*

a  I really enjoy working in television. (As regards …)

_____

b  I worked in the United States for three years. That's my answer to your second question. (In answer to …)

_____

c  I am married and have one child. These are my family commitments. (As far as … are concerned, …)

_____

d  I have never worked on a radio phone-in programme. (As regards …)

_____

e  When does the job start? This is the only question I have. (My only question is …)

_____

## Vocabulary

**Compound nouns**

1 Use a word from each list, A and B. Form compound nouns to complete sentences a–g. Some compounds are written as one word, some as two. Check in a dictionary.

A | break   key   news   search   shop   university   web

B | assistant   board   down   engine   lecturer   reader   site

a The _____ wasn't very helpful. It was five minutes before he served me.

b It's incredible how quickly a _____ can find information on the internet.

c What I'd really like to be is a _____ . I'd enjoy teaching students and researching my subject.

d I was under so much pressure at work last year that I nearly had a nervous

_____ .

e When you're using a computer, make sure the _____ is at the right height or you could get back pains.

f Our college has its own _____ where you can find out about every course on offer.

g Did you see that _____ on Channel One last night? He couldn't stop laughing at one of the stories.

***so* and *such***

2 Rewrite these sentences starting with the words provided. In each case, your answers should include *so* instead of *such* or *such* instead of *so*.

a Maria works so hard that she always gets the highest marks.

Maria is _____ .

b John has such a high IQ that he got into university when he was fourteen.

John's IQ _____ .

c Claudia is such a fast writer that she always finishes first.

Claudia writes _____ .

d I know so many people who wish they hadn't left school at sixteen.

I know _____ .

e Some people have such boring jobs that they can't wait to retire.

Some people's jobs are _____ .

# Listening Part 1

**1** 🔊 **1.8 You will hear people talking in eight different situations. For questions 1–8, choose the best answer (A, B or C).**

1 You hear someone talking about listening to a news programme on the radio.

What does she find most interesting?

A local news stories

B foreign news stories

C the people who read the news

2 You hear someone being interviewed about his reading habits.

On the way to work, which part of the newspaper does he look at first?

A the headlines

B the financial news

C the sports news

3 You hear someone talking about the magazines she reads.

What are her favourite kinds of stories about?

A the homes of people who are rich and famous

B famous people's babies

C future episodes of certain television serials

4 You hear a teenager talking about what he watches on television.

What does he say about himself?

A He is a typical teenager.

B He is good at sports.

C He prefers to be active.

5 You hear someone talking about the internet.

What does he say he is surprised about?

A the fact that people continue to buy newspapers

B the amount of background information you can find

C how quickly you can find out what's happening

6 You hear two people talking about television.

What is the main topic of their conversation?

A a particular film they saw

B the quality of TV programmes

C the choice of TV channels

7 You hear a woman talking about research into early childhood education.

She thinks the findings

A are unsurprising.

B are quite basic.

C will have serious consequences.

8 You hear a man and a woman talking about their plans.

What do they agree to do?

A ask the decorator to come earlier

B speak to the decorator on the phone

C arrange to see the decorator next week

# Vocabulary

**+ Phrasal verbs with *go***

**1** Replace the verbs in *italics* in these sentences with the correct form of *go* and one of the words below.

| after | along with | by | on | through | up |
|---|---|---|---|---|---|

**a** When you're looking forward to something, time *passes* very slowly.

**b** If you *follow* him, you might catch him before he gets on the train.

**c** I don't understand what's wrong with my work. Can you *explain* it again, please?

**d** There was a lot of noise outside our apartment, so we looked out of the window to see what was *happening*.

**e** I'm afraid the price of petrol is likely to *increase* again next month.

**f** Sorry, but I can't *accept* that idea.

# Reading and Use of English Part 5

**1** You are going to read an article on page 49 about radio in rural Africa. For questions 1–6, choose the answer (A, B, C or D) which you think fits best according to the text.

**1** What is the main purpose of the first paragraph of this article?

    **A** to tell the reader about the economy of rural Kenya

    **B** to give background information about a local problem

    **C** to introduce the tea and coffee farmer, Isaac Kinyua

    **D** to illustrate the effects of bad weather conditions

**2** What do we learn about the accident in which the girl was killed?

    **A** People had not been told bad weather was on its way.

    **B** On that day, there had been poor radio reception.

    **C** People in the area had refused to leave their homes.

    **D** Nobody had expected heavy rain at that time of the year.

**3** What is Winfred Chege's attitude to the sound of the radio in the town?

    **A** She is against it because it is very loud.

    **B** She welcomes music being played in public.

    **C** She finds the interruptions annoying.

    **D** She finds the weather news useful.

**4** What does the fact that Winfred Chege puts on a 'heavy sweater' suggest?

    **A** She is finishing work for the day.

    **B** She thinks it is going to rain hard.

    **C** She is preparing herself for the night.

    **D** She thinks the temperature is going to drop.

**5** What was the problem with weather forecasting methods before the arrival of local radio?

    **A** They relied on natural signs.

    **B** They only covered short periods.

    **C** They did not relate to the local area.

    **D** They were based on old-fashioned beliefs.

**6** What is special about the radios given to poor communities?

    **A** They are easy to use.

    **B** They do not use electricity.

    **C** They cost nothing to use.

    **D** They do not need charging.

# Community radio in rural Kenya

The tea and coffee bushes growing on the hillsides around Isaac Kinyua's home in Kenya have long provided him and his family with a livelihood, giving central Kenya an economic advantage over other parts of the country. But the hillsides are also occasionally hit by landslides — one reason Kinyua is now taking the precaution of building a concrete wall on the eastern side of his house, where the land falls steeply to the valley below.

Why now? Because lately, when Kinyua tunes in to his portable radio, he receives weather alerts from the nearby community radio station. One recent warning advised that heavy rains are expected in November and December. 'Disaster preparedness is very important here because of unexpected changes in the weather and landslides,' says Kinyua. Just three years ago, when Kangema had no early warning system, tragedy struck in the form of a landslide that killed a 13-year-old girl and forced hundreds of people to leave their homes.

Kangema RANET, Kangema's local station, attracts listeners with plenty of local music. When Kinyua goes shopping, he is happy to find the radio blaring in Kangema's shopping area. What grabs the attention of Winfred Chege, one of the stallholders, however, is not the music but the occasional interruption for weather forecasts. When the presenter has finished, Chege knows she has to find a way to shelter the food she has been selling all morning because there is likely to be some drizzle a few minutes after midday. She pulls out a plastic cover tucked into one edge of the stall and begins to roll it over the fruit and vegetables on the ground as the skies above begin to darken. She then puts on a heavy sweater and waits for the rain to pass. 'Since the community radio station was established, it has helped us to know what is around us in terms of short- and longer-term weather patterns,' she says. 'Now I know what to do.'

That would have been difficult a few years ago, according to the officer in charge of the radio station, Josphat Kang'ethe, who grew up in this area, one of the rainiest parts of the country.

In the past, people used to rely on traditional weather forecasting methods, including the times at which trees flowered, the snow and fog levels on Mt. Kenya and the varying calls of wild animals. Those forecasts were often long-term and not always accurate. That changed in February 2008, when Kangema RANET went on air, the result of collaboration between the Kenya Meteorological Department and the rural community RANET — Radio and Internet Communication System. Today the station features regular reports from an adjoining weather station. 'Weather readings are taken from the automatic weather station and passed to the radio presenter on duty,' says Kang'ethe. 'The details are then relayed to the community in the local language.'

The Kangema station is part of RANET Kenya and the global RANET project established to transmit vital weather and climate information to rural communities using internet and radio. Kenya now has four such community stations, powered by solar energy, or electricity where available. The stations come with a transmitter and can broadcast in a radius of more than 25 kms. Stations 'are based in areas vulnerable to disasters such as flooding and drought,' says Peter Ambenje, deputy director at the Kenya Meteorological Department. 'We also give the poor communities simple gadgets that use wind-up and solar technology to charge so that they can easily tune in to forecasts.'

In a country where almost half the population lives below the poverty line and natural disasters are seasonal, radio remains the cheapest way for many people to access information.

# Grammar

## Reported speech

**1 Write these sentences in direct speech.**

**a** Andy told his wife to hurry up, adding that they were going to be late.

Andy _____

**b** Sylvia asked him if he thought she should wear her long dress or her short stripy one.

Sylvia _____

**c** Andy suggested she wore her black dress.

Andy _____

**d** Sylvia told him that she couldn't because it was at the dry-cleaner's.

Sylvia _____

**e** Andy said he didn't care what she wore, but that if they were late, he might lose his job.

Andy _____

**2 Report the following conversations, using the verbs in brackets. Use conjunctions to join short sentences together where possible and make any other necessary changes. The first one is done as an example.**

**a** Paul    Would you like to come to my party next Saturday? (invite) Pete and John are coming, so there'll be some people there that you know. (add)
*Paul invited Delia to his party the following Saturday, adding that Pete and John were coming, so there would be some people there that she knew.*

     Delia    Yes, I'd love to. (say) What time does it start? (ask)

     Paul    About ten, but you can come when you like. (reply)

**b** Delia    I've been invited to Paul's party. (say)

     Angie    When is it? (ask)

     Delia    On Saturday. (reply) I don't want to go, but I couldn't say no. (add)

     Angie    Why don't you phone him on Saturday and say you don't feel well? (suggest)

**c** Mum    Now, don't make too much noise. (warn) I don't want any complaints from the neighbours. (add)

     Paul    I won't. (promise)

**d** Pete    Why didn't you come to Paul's party, Delia? (ask)

     Delia    Oh, because everyone said it would be boring. (reply)

     Pete    I really enjoyed it. (say) It didn't finish till after four. Angie and John were there. (add)

**3 Rewrite these sentences in reported speech. Choose the most appropriate reporting verb from this list, using each verb once only.**

| insist    remind    suggest    tell    warn |
| --- |

**a** 'Don't speak with your mouth full, John!'

John's mother _____.

**b** 'Remember to get your father a birthday present, Laura.'

Laura's mother _____.

**c** 'Don't cross the road here, Tom! It's not safe.'

The man _____.

**d** 'You really must let me pay.'

David _____.

**e** 'Let's try that new Chinese restaurant in King Street.'

Susie _____

# Reading and Use of English Part 2

1 For questions 1–8, read the text below and think of the word which best fits each gap. Use only one word in each gap. There is an example at the beginning (0).

## Mini Televisions

Scott Newman loves his pocket-size TV, **(0)** ___which___ he mainly watches in bed. 'I only watch programmes which last about an hour, as any longer strains my eyes. I use it for entertainment, but it is also good for keeping **(1)** _____ with current affairs. The main problem is that it is not loud **(2)** _____ , even with headphones. The reception is good **(3)** _____ long as nothing moves in front of the aerial.' Scott admits that he is a gadget man, but does not regret buying the TV as he uses it every day.

Paul Hardcastle **(4)** _____ owned a pocket TV for several years. 'I use it mostly in the bathroom. I wanted to use it outdoors, **(5)** _____ in bright light you cannot see the picture.' Paul believes this sort of TV could be improved **(6)** _____ the screen was bigger and it didn't use up batteries **(7)** _____ quickly: he can only get half an hour's viewing **(8)** _____ the batteries run out.

# Writing Part 1

1 Choose the correct word or phrase to complete the following sentences.

a Today, fewer and fewer people are buying newspapers. *However / On balance*, more people are reading the news online.

b In the past, the role of a newspaper was to report the news, *although / whereas* today its role is to entertain.

c I hardly ever read newspapers now. *By contrast / In fact*, I can't remember the last time I actually bought one.

d It's much easier to watch the news on TV. *By contrast / On the other hand*, there's something satisfying about turning the pages of a newspaper.

e You may think I have no interest in the news. *Nevertheless / On the contrary*, I am fascinated by what's going on in the world.

f My brother always reads the sports reports. *Apart from that / As well as that*, there's nothing he's really interested in.

2 Rewrite the second sentence in each of these pairs so as to avoid repetition.

a Local radio is a brilliant invention. Local radio is cheap to produce and gets large audiences.

_____

b I can think of two advantages radio has over television. The first advantage is that you can do something while you are listening.

_____

c There are many interesting radio programmes about science and technology. In my opinion, programmes about science and technology are interesting and informative.

_____

d We arranged to meet outside the station at 6 o'clock. I hope I can get to the station by 6 o'clock.

_____

# Unit 9 | Around us

## Listening Part 4

1 🔊 1.9 **You will hear part of a radio interview with an environmentalist, Daniel James, about the Eden Project. For questions 1–7, choose the best answer (A, B or C).**

1 What interests Daniel about visitors to the Eden Project?

 A They mainly come from other parts of the UK.

 B Around a third have never been to Cornwall before.

 C They are happy to pay to visit it.

2 What does Daniel say about the conservatories?

 A They are round in shape.

 B They will need to be replaced in 25 years' time.

 C They are made of two different materials.

3 What does the Humid Tropics Biome mainly contain?

 A plants which bear edible fruit

 B plants from tropical forests

 C plants used in construction

4 In what way is the third biome different?

 A It contains plants from Asia and Australia.

 B It isn't covered.

 C It contains more varied plants.

5 What is the main aim of the Eden Project?

 A to conserve endangered plant species

 B to study how plants and trees grow

 C to show the connection between plants and people

6 What kind of people does the Eden Project especially want to attract?

 A people who haven't got much interest in environmental issues

 B people who are interested in the environment

 C people who belong to environmental groups

7 What does Daniel say about the majority of the people who visit the Eden Project?

 A They arrive at 9 a.m. or after 2.30 p.m.

 B They don't have time to look at all the exhibits.

 C They spend three to four hours there.

# Vocabulary

**Dependent prepositions**

**1** Complete these sentences with an appropriate preposition from this list.

| about | against | between | in | on | to |
|---|---|---|---|---|---|

a The Eden Project appeals _____ both adults and children.

b Eden's creators believed _____ the project so strongly that many gave up good jobs to be able to work on it.

c The Project has had a positive effect _____ the local economy.

d Some people were opposed _____ the Project, which was partly funded by lottery money.

e Local companies also invested _____ the scheme.

f Many local people have complained _____ the high admission price, which is comparable _____ the price of a ticket to see a top football match.

g All imported plants are put into quarantine to ensure _____ the spread of disease.

h Although there isn't a ban _____ cars, they would prefer people to use public transport to get to the Project.

i The Eden Project hopes to make an important contribution _____ our understanding of the relationship _____ people and plants.

j A visit to the Eden Project is a good alternative _____ a day at the beach.

**⊕ Collocations with *make* and *take***

**2** Complete these sentences with *make* or *take* in the correct form and one of these prepositions.

| at | for | from | in | of | off | with |
|---|---|---|---|---|---|---|

a Their mobile wasn't working so they couldn't _____ contact _____ anyone to say they would be late.

b Janet is _____ a good recovery _____ her injuries.

c I was really nervous about my driving test, so I tried to read a magazine to _____ my mind _____ it.

d Can you _____ room _____ another person in the back? I said I'd give Emma a lift, too.

e When she joined the club, she _____ friends _____ the other members very quickly.

f If the team plays well, he _____ all the credit _____ it. This makes the other players angry.

g Parents should _____ an interest _____ their children's progress at school.

h It was his first holiday in five years, and he was going to _____ the most _____ it.

i Could you _____ a look _____ my ankle? I think I might have broken it.

**1** You are going to read an article about predicting earthquakes. For questions 1–6, choose the answer (A, B, C or D) which you think fits best according to the text.

# Predicting earthquakes

unit 9 around us

1 Since the beginning of recorded history, virtually every culture in the world has reported observations of unusual animal behaviour prior to earthquakes and, to a lesser extent, volcanic eruptions, but conventional science has never been able to adequately explain 5 the phenomenon.

Nevertheless, the Chinese and Japanese have used such observations for hundreds of years as an important part of their earthquake warning systems.

Most significantly, on 4 February 1975, the Chinese 10 successfully evacuated the city of Haicheng several hours before a 7.3 magnitude earthquake, saving nearly 90,000 lives. This was based primarily on observations of unusual animal behaviour.

Helmut Tributsch's classic work on the subject of 15 earthquakes and unusual animal behaviour – *When the Snakes Awake* – details numerous consistent accounts of the phenomenon from all over the world. However, although these behaviour patterns are very well-documented, most American specialists do not take them very seriously. 20 In fact, most conventional geologists do not believe that there are any earthquake prediction techniques which perform any better than chance; this includes unusual animal behaviour. In fact, the notion that odd animal behaviour can help people predict earthquakes is 25 perceived by most traditional geologists in the West as folklore, and is often treated as seriously as sightings of ghosts, Elvis Presley, and the Loch Ness Monster.

Unusual behaviour is difficult to define, and 30 determining if there is a typical behaviour pattern is not a simple, clear-cut process, although there are some distinct patterns which have emerged. An example of this, which has often been reported, is an 35 intense fear that appears to make some animals cry or bark for hours, and others run away in panic. Equally typical is the phenomenon of wild animals losing their usual fear of people.

40 Although the majority of accounts relate to dogs and cats, there are also many stories about other types of animal in the wild, on farms, and in zoos. Unusual behaviour has been reported in many other animal 45 species as well, including fish, reptiles, and even insects. This strange behaviour can occur at any time in advance of a quake – from weeks to seconds.

A number of theories have been proposed to explain this phenomenon, and what the signals that the 50 animals are picking up on might be. Because many animals possess auditory capacities beyond the human range, it has been suggested that some animals may be reacting to ultrasound emitted as *microseisms from rock breaking below the 55 earth's surface.

Another possibility is fluctuations in the earth's magnetic field. Because some animals have a sensitivity to variations in the earth's magnetic field (usually as a means of orientation), and since 60 variations in the magnetic field occur near the epicentres of earthquakes, it has been suggested that this is what the animals are picking up on.

Other mysterious phenomena are often connected with earthquakes. The regular eruptions of geysers 65 have been interrupted. Water levels in wells have been reported to change, or the water itself has become cloudy. Magnets have been said to lose their power temporarily. Many people report that there is suddenly an inexplicable stillness 70 in the air, and that all around them becomes completely silent. Strange lights are often seen glowing from the earth, and unusual fogs have been reported. These phenomena are all consistent with the notion that the odd 75 animal behaviour may result from changes in the earth's electromagnetic field. More puzzling is the fact that a number of people even claim to have sighted UFOs hovering around earthquake sites.

Currently, Western science does not have any 80 reliable means of forecasting earthquakes. Any clues that may be used to help us predict when and where the next quake is coming should be approached with an open mind.

> **Glossary**
> microseism: a weak, persistently-recurring earth tremor

1 What does the writer say about the occurrence of unusual animal behaviour before earthquakes?

  A It does not happen everywhere in the world.

  B Many countries use it to predict earthquakes.

  C It is equally common before volcanic eruptions.

  D There is no generally approved scientific explanation for it.

2 According to the writer of the article, most conventional geologists

  A use unusual animal behaviour to predict earthquakes.

  B think *When the Snakes Awake* is well researched.

  C believe there is no sure way of predicting earthquakes.

  D support scientific study of unusual animal behaviour.

3 What does the writer say about how animals behave before an earthquake?

  A Both wild and domesticated animals show unusual behaviour.

  B Cats and dogs show more unusual behaviour than other animals.

  C All animals become frightened of people.

  D Some pets run away from home.

4 What is a possible cause of animals' strange behaviour?

  A They feel the earth beginning to move.

  B They sense changes in the earth's magnetic field.

  C They are highly sensitive to magnets.

  D They hear loud sounds below the earth's surface.

5 How does the writer react to claims that UFOs have been seen around earthquake sites?

  A He thinks the claims are probably true.

  B He is surprised by the claims.

  C He finds the claims difficult to explain.

  D He is concerned about the claims.

6 What is the main point the writer of the article is trying to make?

  A More studies need to be done on animal behaviour and earthquakes.

  B Western scientists should listen to new ideas about how to predict earthquakes.

  C People who say they can predict earthquakes are not of sound mind.

  D It is impossible to predict when earthquakes will occur.

## Vocabulary

➕ **Word building**    1 **Complete this table with words made from these root verbs.**

| Verb | Noun | Verb | Noun |
|------|------|------|------|
| observe | | behave | |
| predict | | perform | |
| define | | occur | |
| explain | | suggest | |
| react | | fluctuate | |
| vary | | erupt | |

# Grammar

## Relative clauses

**1** Decide whether the relative clauses in the following sentences are defining (they contain essential information) or non-defining (they contain non-essential information). If the clause is non-defining, add commas.

   **a** The word 'smog' which was coined in the early 20th century combines the words 'smoke' and 'fog'.

   **b** In the late 19th century, London which was known as 'The Big Smoke' suffered almost constant foggy conditions.

   **c** At that time fog was mainly caused by the smoke which came from the coal fires burning in thousands of homes.

   **d** The worst recorded London smog was in 1952 when 4,000 people died in the week that it lasted.

   **e** Because of the poor visibility which was often less than one metre dozens died in road accidents.

   **f** These days smog which particularly affects people who have respiratory problems is mainly caused when fuel emissions from cars react with sunlight in humid, still, atmospheric conditions.

   **g** The countries whose industrial economies have accelerated almost overnight, namely China and India, have the worst air pollution.

   **h** The industries which pollute the most are those which use fossil fuels like coal.

   **i** To date, the US president who has done most to improve $CO_2$ emissions in that country is President Obama.

**2** Complete these sentences with appropriate relative pronouns. There may be more than one possible answer. Add commas if the clause is non-defining.

   **a** The 10.05 from London to Norwich _____ is due to arrive at Platform 1 will call at Colchester, Ipswich and Norwich.

   **b** We'll have the party next Friday _____ is the day _____ he comes out of hospital.

   **c** The golden eagle _____ eggs are stolen by unscrupulous collectors is now an endangered species.

   **d** What's the name of the girl _____ got married to Chris Small? Is it Louise?

   **e** Can you think of any reason _____ he might have done it?

   **f** I don't know of any restaurants _____ you can get a decent meal for under £15.

   **g** What's the name of that singer _____ record was number one last month? The one _____ writes his own songs.

   **h** United's second goal _____ was scored in the final minute won them the cup.

   **i** Sally's going out with someone _____ she met at Jason's party.

   **j** Not surprisingly, we never got back the things _____ we'd reported stolen.

   **k** We'll be staying at the Seaview Hotel _____ is on the seafront.

   **l** The best time to go to Scotland is June _____ the weather is warmer.

   **m** I've decided I don't like the shoes _____ I bought on Saturday.

   **n** The Hilton is expensive _____ is what you'd expect. After all, it is a five-star hotel.

   **o** The girl over there _____ is talking to John used to go to my school.

**3** In which sentences above could the relative pronoun be omitted?

**4** Rewrite these formal sentences more informally, leaving out the relative pronoun where possible.

   **a** The guest house at which we stayed when we were in Prague was right in the city centre.

   _____

   **b** The couple with whom we shared our table at lunch were from Poland.

   _____

   **c** The travel agency through which we booked our holiday was excellent.

   _____

   **d** The tour, about which we had heard so much, was definitely worth going on.

   _____

   **e** The audio guide, without which we would have been lost, was available in several languages.

   _____

   **f** The holiday, to which we'd looked forward so much, was over too soon.

   _____

# Reading and Use of English Part 3

1 For questions 1–8, read the text below. Use the word given in capitals at the end of some of the lines to form a word that fits in the gap in the same line. There is an example at the beginning (0).

## ORBIS - The Flying Eye Hospital

ORBIS was the idea of Dr David Paton. After travelling (0) _extensively_ throughout the developing world during the 1970s, Dr Paton observed that the high costs of tuition, (1) _____ travel and accommodation prevented most (2) _____ staff in these countries from participating in overseas training programmes. His solution was a mobile eye surgery hospital. Thanks to the (3) _____ of an out-of-service DC-8 plane, which was converted into a fully functional teaching hospital, doctors trained in the latest techniques were able to pass on their surgical (4) _____ and skills through hands-on training and lectures. Since its first programme in 1982, the ORBIS Flying Eye Hospital has travelled to 78 countries and saved the (5) _____ of millions. By training local doctors and eye care workers, who in turn teach their colleagues, ORBIS is (6) _____ the capabilities of local healthcare communities in (7) _____ prevention and (8) _____ . In 2011, ORBIS began building a new Flying Eye Hospital, which will include state-of-the-art technology.

EXTEND

NATION
MEDICINE

DONATE

KNOW

SEE

STRONG
BLIND
TREAT

# Writing Part 2 – Report

1 Rewrite these ideas more formally using the passive.

a If you made parking in the town centre more expensive, it might encourage people to leave their cars at home.

_____
_____

b You could introduce a park-and-ride scheme. You could build a car park outside the town with cheap parking, and you could provide free transport into the town centre.

_____
_____

c You should install more bicycle racks, where people can leave their bikes safely.

_____
_____

d You could ban cars from going into the town centre altogether and only allow bikes, taxis and buses.

_____
_____

e If you implemented the suggested changes, you would reduce the amount of pollution in the town centre.

_____
_____

## Reading and Use of English Part 7

1 You are going to read an article about four entrepreneurs who put forward their business ideas to potential investors on a TV show called *Dragons' Den*. For questions 1–10, choose from the entrepreneurs (A–D). The entrepreneurs may be chosen more than once.

# Entrepreneurs

*Four entrepreneurs talk about their experiences on 'Dragons' Den'.*

### A James Halliburton: The Illoom Balloon

1 The Dragons saw the business potential of Mr Halliburton's invention – a glowing balloon which kept keys afloat when they fell into water – and he initially accepted a £200,000 offer for a 25% stake in his company. However, Mr
5 Halliburton later changed his mind because when he was testing out his invention, he came up with an even better idea. 'When I saw how excited my next-door neighbour's young sons were about an illuminated balloon, I knew there was an opportunity to tap into that with an innovative new
10 product. It left me in no doubt that I could do it on my own, safe in the knowledge that I had an even bigger project in the pipeline.' The Illoom Balloon is simply a reinforced balloon fitted with a tiny LED light inside, which glows brightly when it is inflated. Mr Halliburton continued, 'I took a gamble by
15 not going with the Dragons' cash, but it has really paid off.'

### B Kirsty Henshaw: Freedom Desserts

Kirsty Henshaw secured a deal after impressing the investors on *Dragons' Den*. Kirsty decided to create her own range of dairy-free frozen desserts when she discovered that her son, Jacob, had an intolerance to dairy products. She said: 'It
20 started with my little ice-cream maker. Jacob seemed to love the desserts, which was my main aim. Then I just thought that maybe it could work as a business as well.' Kirsty admitted she had been anxious about facing the judges. 'Walking into the Den was nerve-racking,' she said. 'But hearing the
25 Dragons compliment me and my product made up for all the hard work. When I first set out, it was very hard. I lived with my mum and had two jobs to save money to fund my dream. This opportunity has made me even more determined to keep on working hard to make the brand a success.'

### C Shaun Pulfrey: The Tangle Teezer

30 *Dragons' Den* reject, Shaun Pulfrey, has had his innovative hairbrush snapped up by a well-known pharmaceutical company. The device, designed to smooth tangled hair easily, should make the hairdresser a good profit. Mr Pulfrey was turned down by the Dragons, who advised him to abandon
35 his idea, saying it was not a worthwhile business project. Mr Pulfrey said: 'I just made a comment about one of the panelists colouring her hair to show how useful the product could be on highlighted hair. The fact that she denied her hair was coloured made me lose all hope.' Despite leaving the
40 show with no investment, he said, 'The whole experience has been instrumental in my success because of the exposure it gave me and my product, but the actual success of the product has been driven by its ability to do what it says it on the pack. I knew there was a market for the Tangle Teezer.'

### D Natalie Ellis: The Road Refresher Water Bowl

45 Natalie Ellis appeared on the show asking for £120,000 to help export her non-spill dog water bowl to America. When she tearfully admitted that her previous business had failed after she had a stroke, aged just 37, she won sympathy from the Dragons but no investment. But viewers were
50 impressed, and sales of the bowl have soared since the show. Natalie was an unusual contestant on *Dragons' Den*: unlike most, she did not apply. 'Two researchers approached me at an awards ceremony and asked me to go on,' she says. 'I didn't need investment, I just wanted expertise. The
55 story was picked up by the American press and I am now in talks with US retailers. I want to grow my business over there then sell it,' adds Natalie, who moves to Chicago at the end of the month.

**Which person**

| | |
|---|---|
| says they were interested in the advice the investors could give them? | 1 |
| suggests they are pleased they didn't accept the investors' offer? | 2 |
| mentions the sacrifices they had to make? | 3 |
| says that going on the programme was useful? | 4 |
| mentions a distressing experience? | 5 |
| mentions taking a risk? | 6 |
| says they never lost faith in their idea? | 7 |
| explains how they were inspired by a health problem? | 8 |
| describes how they felt during the programme? | 9 |
| mentions a mistake they made? | 10 |

# Vocabulary

➕ **Words often confused**

**1 Choose the correct word in *italics* in these sentences.**

1 a My favourite *desert / dessert* is apple pie and ice-cream.

  b The cactus is one of the few plants which can survive in the *desert / dessert*.

2 a I always get embarrassed when someone pays me a *compliment / complement*.

  b Mint sauce is the perfect *compliment / complement* to roast lamb.

3 a James didn't realize that the car in front was *stationery / stationary* and crashed into it.

  b We need to get some more *stationery / stationary*. We've run out of writing paper and envelopes.

4 a Modern farming techniques have had an adverse *affect / effect* on the environment.

  b Lack of investment did not *affect / effect* Shaun's determination to succeed.

5 a Generally, smaller cars are more *economic / economical* to run than larger cars.

  b The current *economic / economical* situation is improving slowly.

6 a In *principle / principal*, the idea is good but it may be expensive to put into practice.

  b One of the *principle / principal* reasons why new businesses fail is lack of experience.

➕ **Phrasal verbs with *keep***

**2 Choose the correct alternative in *italics* to make an appropriate phrasal verb with *keep*.**

a Sonia kept *on / up* working right through her pregnancy.

b We'll have the wedding reception outside as long as the rain keeps *out / off*.

c He walked so fast that I couldn't keep up *with / in* him.

d When you're on a diet, you have to keep *off / out* fatty foods and alcohol if you want to lose weight.

e You've done really well. Don't stop now. Keep *on / up* the good work!

f The best way to keep *on / up* with what's happening in the world is to watch the news or read the newspaper every day.

➕ **Expressions with *take***

**3 Complete these sentences with an appropriate noun from the list below.**

| advice blame dislike gamble interest offence seat |
|---|

a My boss admitted he had taken a / an _____ by offering me the job but that it had more than paid off.

b I absolutely refuse to take the _____ for something I did not do!

c Parents should always take a / an _____ in their children's hobbies.

d Please take a / an _____, Ms Jones. Mr Smith will be with you shortly.

e Take my _____ and live life as you want to, not as other people want you to.

f I have no idea why, but I took an instant _____ to Aaron's new girlfriend.

g What do you think of this new recipe? I promise I won't take _____ if you say you don't like it.

# Grammar

## Wishes and regrets

1  Complete these sentences with the correct form of the verbs in brackets.

a  I wish I _____ (have) straight hair!

b  I'm so tired. I wish I _____ (not / go) to bed so late last night.

c  I wish I _____ (can) afford to run a car like that.

d  I wish you _____ (put) your dirty socks in the laundry basket and not drop them on the floor!

e  Darren wishes he _____ (remember) to buy his girlfriend a birthday present.

f  I wish I _____ (not / live) in the countryside. There's nothing to do!

g  Tony wished he _____ (work) harder at school and _____ (get) some qualifications.

h  Susan felt sick and wished she _____ (not eat) so much chocolate.

i  Peter wishes he _____ (be) taller so that he could see better at football matches.

j  I wish Alison _____ (hurry up)! I'm fed up with waiting.

k  Don't you sometimes wish you _____ (not / get married) so young?

l  I wish it _____ (stop) raining. I want to play tennis.

m  Mary wishes she _____ (learn) to swim when she was young.

n  I wish I _____ (listen) to my brother's advice.

## I'd rather

2  Complete these sentences with one of these verbs in an appropriate form. You will need to make some of the verbs negative.

| arrive | call | drive | eat | go | have |
|--------|------|-------|-----|-----|------|
| invite | play | visit | | | |

a  I think I'd rather _____ to the cinema than rent a DVD.

b  I'd rather we _____ out tonight for a change. I'm tired of cooking.

c  I'd rather _____ football than watch it any day.

d  'Would you like another sandwich?' 'I'd rather _____ a piece of cake.'

e  I'd rather you _____ Patrick to the party. I don't like him very much.

f  Would you rather I _____ you after eleven? I don't want to wake you up.

g  I'd rather _____ than be a passenger, wouldn't you?

h  I'd rather _____ too early. I hate being the first person there.

i  We'd rather you _____ us next month. We're both very busy at the moment.

## It's time

3  Read these situations and write an appropriate sentence beginning with It's time.

a  It's half past seven. You get up at half past seven every day. What do you say to yourself?

   It's time _____ .

b  You are thirty years old and you still live with your parents. Your friend thinks you should get your own place. What does he say?

   Don't you think it's time _____ ?

c  Your mother asked you to put the lamb in the oven at twelve o'clock. It's twelve o'clock now. What does your sister say to you?

   Isn't it time _____ ?

d  Your doctor thinks you should have a holiday. What does she say to you?

   It's time _____ .

# Reading and Use of English Part 4

1 For questions 1–6, complete the second sentence so that it has a similar meaning to the first sentence, using the word given. Do not change the word given. You must use between two and five words, including the word given. Here is an example (0).

**EXAMPLE**

0 Jason adds up figures well for someone his age.

**GOOD**

Jason ___*is good at adding up*___ figures for someone his age.

1 It's a pity you didn't tell me earlier.

**WISH**

I _____ me earlier.

2 I would prefer you not to smoke, if you don't mind.

**RATHER**

I _____ smoke, if you don't mind.

3 I'm not sorry I chose nursing as a career.

**REGRET**

I _____ nursing as a career.

4 Some people have complained about the noise.

**SEVERAL**

There _____ about the noise.

5 Have you decided what you would like for dinner?

**MIND**

Have you _____ what you would like for dinner?

6 The plane left on time although the weather was bad.

**TOOK**

The plane _____ the bad weather.

# Vocabulary

**⊕ Phrasal verbs with *make***

1 Use a dictionary to check the meaning of these phrasal verbs if you need to. Then complete the gaps in these sentences with an appropriate verb in an appropriate form.

> make into    make out    make up    make up for    make up to sb

a The compensation we received from the travel company only slightly _____ our disastrous holiday.

b I'm so sorry I forgot your birthday. I'll _____ it _____ you, I promise!

c Sam and Anna _____ their spare bedroom _____ a study. We could do the same.

d Why do doctors have such illegible handwriting? You can never _____ what they've written.

e Andy arrived late as usual. He _____ some excuse about the train being late.

**Compound adjectives**

2 The answers to these clues are hidden in the grid. Words can go across or down.

a Someone who cares about others is kind-_____ .

b Someone who can see something clearly only if it is very close to them is _____-sighted.

c A person who has a very high opinion of themselves is big-_____ .

d Another word for attractive to describe a person is good-_____ .

e Someone who is relaxed and happy to accept things is _____-going.

f Memories which bring pleasure mixed with sadness are bitter-_____ .

g A change which is likely to have a lot of significant effects is _____-reaching

h A person whose skin is brown from exposure to the sun is sun-_____ .

i The opposite of sensitive for a person is _____-skinned.

j The opposite of modern is old-_____ .

k Another word for transparent is _____-through.

l The opposite of made-to-measure is _____-to-wear.

| R | K | Z | S | W | E | E | T | P | R | S | E | E |
|---|---|---|---|---|---|---|---|---|---|---|---|---|
| J | E | W | H | E | A | D | E | D | S | C | X | L |
| S | F | O | O | D | L | O | O | K | I | N | G | A |
| E | F | A | S | H | I | O | N | E | D | M | O | T |
| A | J | I | R | F | T | R | E | T | C | H | Y | A |
| S | C | G | E | A | I | E | K | H | R | A | C | N |
| Y | M | I | A | R | Y | E | T | I | O | R | O | N |
| E | Q | N | D | I | N | H | B | C | E | D | L | E |
| K | I | A | Y | A | E | F | I | K | V | U | D | D |
| A | O | L | I | L | C | R | S | H | O | R | T | E |
| H | E | A | R | T | E | D | Y | E | B | D | A | S |

3 Complete these sentences with an adjective related to the word in brackets.

a Most _____ (innovation) ideas are the result of trying to find a solution to a problem.

b The most _____ (success) ideas are often the simplest.

c When colour TVs first came onto the market, they were expensive, but now they are very _____ (afford).

d You don't need to be particularly _____ (artist) to design a new product.

e _____ (number) inventions are patented every year.

## Listening Part 2

1 🔊 1.10 **You will hear a man called Andrew South giving a talk about how we will travel in the future. For questions 1–10, complete the sentences with a word or short phrase.**

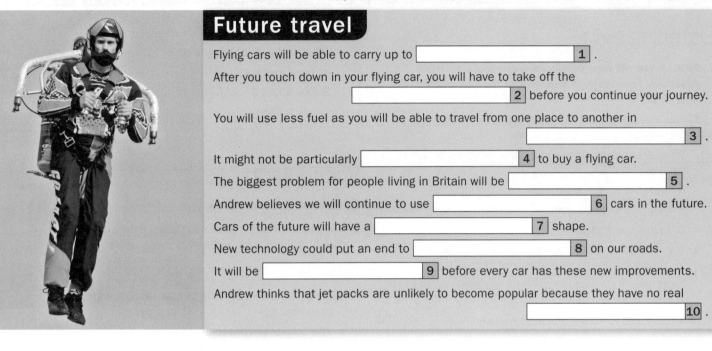

### Future travel

Flying cars will be able to carry up to [_____ **1** ].

After you touch down in your flying car, you will have to take off the [_____ **2** ] before you continue your journey.

You will use less fuel as you will be able to travel from one place to another in [_____ **3** ].

It might not be particularly [_____ **4** ] to buy a flying car.

The biggest problem for people living in Britain will be [_____ **5** ].

Andrew believes we will continue to use [_____ **6** ] cars in the future.

Cars of the future will have a [_____ **7** ] shape.

New technology could put an end to [_____ **8** ] on our roads.

It will be [_____ **9** ] before every car has these new improvements.

Andrew thinks that jet packs are unlikely to become popular because they have no real [_____ **10** ].

## Writing Part 2 – Review

1 **Read the book review below. For questions 1–7 choose the word or phrase that is incorrect.**

'The Small Assassin' is a short story **(1)** *written / described / penned* by the American author Ray Bradbury. Ray Bradbury wrote many science fiction and fantasy novels and short stories, but this one made a **(2)** *large / big / strong* impression on me.

It **(3)** *tells / relates / gives* the story of a happily-married couple who have a baby. The wife, Alice, almost dies giving birth and develops a hatred for the child, who she is convinced is trying to kill her. David, her husband, thinks his wife is imagining things, but then he starts to think differently when he finds toys mysteriously left at the top of the stairs. One day, he comes home from work to find his wife lying dead at the foot of the stairs. She has tripped over a toy at the top. The doctor who delivered the child doesn't believe his concerns. He thinks it is just a coincidence. What **(4)** *happens / comes / appears* next makes him wonder if they were right after all.

I would recommend this story because it is **(5)** *compulsive / gripping / riveting* from **(6)** *start to finish / opening to closing / beginning to end*. I **(7)** *assure / guarantee / promise* that if you read it you will want to read more by this author.

2 **Rearrange the letters to form words to complete these sentences.**

a A person who writes novels is a *nleiotvs*. _____

b An *arytboohguaip* is the story of a person's life written by that person. _____

c A *oltp* is the series of events that form the story of a novel, play, film, etc. _____

d A *ctphera* is a separate section of a book, usually with a number or title. _____

e The opposite of 'factual' is *fnliicoat*. _____

## Listening Part 1

**1** 🔊 **1.11 You will hear people talking in eight different situations. For questions 1–8, choose the best answer (A, B or C).**

**1** You hear a woman talking about people of different nationalities.

What did she use to assume about people who used gestures?

**A** that they were foreign

**B** that they were strange

**C** that it was normal

**2** You hear someone being interviewed about learning a language.

What does the speaker say about the family he lived with?

**A** They always spoke to him in English.

**B** They were teachers at the local college.

**C** He learned a lot of Thai from them.

**3** You hear someone talking about her oldest friend.

How do the two friends keep in touch?

**A** by writing to each other

**B** by phoning each other every month

**C** by visiting each other several times a year

**4** You overhear two friends talking about an interview.

What does the man tell the woman to avoid?

**A** blinking

**B** staring

**C** eye contact

**5** You hear a man talking about his first lie.

What happened when the speaker and his mother returned from shopping?

**A** His mother discovered the medicine.

**B** He hid the medicine in a cupboard.

**C** He took more of the medicine.

**6** You overhear a conversation between two people.

What situation are they talking about?

**A** getting stuck in rush hour traffic

**B** being stopped by the police

**C** a car breakdown

**7** You hear a novelist talking about her work.

What were her views about it?

**A** that it was unlikely to be published

**B** that an agent would find it interesting

**C** that it needed to be rewritten

**8** You hear a man asking for information.

What is the man trying to do?

**A** buy a computer

**B** buy books

**C** join a library

## Vocabulary

➕ **Phrasal verbs with *stick***

**1** Replace the verbs in *italics* in these sentences with the correct form of *stick* and one of these words.

| at | by | out of | to | together | up for |
| --- | --- | --- | --- | --- | --- |

**a** When I was little, my big brother always *helped and protected* me.

**b** The employees are realizing that, if they *are united*, they can win an increased pay offer.

**c** I really admire the way she has *continued to work hard at* that job even though she's found it really tough.

**d** I'll always *help and support* my children whatever they do.

**e** That's my story and I'm *not changing* it.

**f** He tore his trousers on a nail that was *protruding from* the wall.

***say, speak, talk, tell***

**2** Complete these sentences with the correct form of one of these four verbs: *say*, *speak*, *talk*, *tell*.

**a** I asked my father if I could borrow his car and he _____ yes.

**b** Did I ever _____ you the story of how I broke my leg?

**c** I'd love to be able to _____ Italian. It's such a romantic language.

**d** Apparently, George Washington never _____ a lie.

**e** There's no point in being shy. You've just got to _____ your mind.

**f** He just wouldn't stop _____ . In the end, I put the phone down.

**Adjectives with similar meanings**

**3** Do the words in *italics* in these sentences have positive or negative meanings? Write P or N in the spaces.

a We've got a really *nosey* next-door neighbour. _____

b My brother's a pretty *determined* sort of person. _____

c He seems *overconfident* to me. _____

d She's very interesting, but I find her a rather *cold* person. _____

e He wore *cheap* shoes for the interview. _____

f A few of the students in my class are really *lazy*. _____

g He's *well-built* for a man of his age. _____

**4** Complete this table with the appropriate words from **3**. The first one is done as an example.

| More positive | More negative |
|---|---|
| a _curious_ | nosey |
| b easy-going | _____ |
| c _____ | fat |
| d inexpensive | _____ |
| e outgoing | _____ |
| f reserved | _____ |
| g _____ | ruthless |

**Confusing verbs**

**5** Complete these sentences with the correct form of one of the verbs below.

| expect    hope    look forward to    wait |

a I _____ to get my exam results any day now. I just _____ I've passed.

b The train was delayed because of an accident. We had to _____ for nearly two hours.

c Are you _____ starting your new job?

d My sister _____ us for lunch. We mustn't keep her _____ .

e Good luck at the weekend. I _____ everything goes well.

f I'm really _____ my summer holiday this year. I just can't _____ for the end of term.

**1** You are going to read an article about unidentified flying objects (UFOs). Six sentences have been removed from the article. Choose from the sentences A–G the one which fits each gap (1–6). There is one extra sentence which you do not need to use.

# UFO SIGHTINGS

1 Visitors from space are the subject of many 20th-century fairy tales, yet millions of normal people sincerely believe that they are real. **1** But is there any real proof?

The first recorded case of this kind was in the 1950s, when 5 George Adamski claimed that he had been given rides in flying saucers belonging to people from Venus, Mars and Saturn. **2** Another early case of alien kidnapping took place a few years later in 1961, when an American couple, Betty and Barney Hill, saw a UFO while driving home one 10 night in New Hampshire. The couple stopped to observe the UFO through binoculars and thought they could see people aboard. To escape from what they were sure was an alien spaceship, they took the back roads and arrived home two hours late. A week later, Mrs Hill began to 15 dream that they had not escaped, but had been taken on board the spaceship and medically examined. **3** She even described how she had seen a star map, marked with the aliens' trade routes.

**4** This extraordinary event happened in a small town in 20 Arizona, when a team of woodcutters who were working in a remote forest area returned home with a strange story of how one of their group had disappeared in the forest. They had, apparently, seen their friend Travis Walton knocked unconscious by a blue-green light from a flying saucer.

25 They found this so terrifying that they did not stay to see what happened next but drove off as fast as they could. **5** He said he had woken up on the UFO and found himself surrounded by creatures with no hair and with half-formed faces. These 'people' then put a mask over his face 30 and he fell asleep again. He claims that he remembered nothing else until he awoke in the forest near to where he had disappeared.

At the time, his story received national publicity, some people calling it the most impressive case of its kind. 35 **6** Now, three decades later, and despite the fact that there is absolutely no hard evidence that the earth has ever received visitors from space, the results of several American surveys indicate that the majority of people are convinced that there are such things as UFOs.

40 This suggests that people want flying saucers to exist, maybe because as human beings we need to believe that we are not alone in the universe or that there are superior beings capable of showing us how to survive in an increasingly hostile world. This probably explains the lasting 45 popularity of films and books involving UFOs and aliens of all kinds. Two of the most well-known, *ET* and *Close Encounters of the Third Kind*, were massive box office hits.

**A** Five days later, the missing woodcutter returned home with an equally amazing story.

**B** Under hypnosis, she gave a psychiatrist a detailed account of events on the spaceship.

**C** Frank Fontaine disappeared for a week during December 1979, apparently kidnapped by a UFO.

**D** Fourteen years later, in 1975, one of the most famous 'kidnappings' of all took place in the USA.

**E** Some people maintain that they have been visited or even kidnapped by aliens.

**F** However, an organization that investigates UFO cases concluded that the story was a hoax.

**G** He said that two beautiful young women had taken him to cities on the far side of the moon.

# Vocabulary

## ➕ Word building

**1** **What are the nouns related to these adjectives from the article?**

a amazing _amazement_        e national _____

b beautiful _____        f real _____

c famous _____        g superior _____

d hostile _____        h terrifying _____

**2** **What are the nouns related to these verbs from the article?**

a believe _belief_        e exist _____

b conclude _____        f indicate _____

c convince _____        g observe _____

d disappear _____        h suggest _____

# Reading and Use of English Part 2

For questions 1–8, read the text below and think of the word which best fits each gap. Use only one word in each gap. There is an example at the beginning (0).

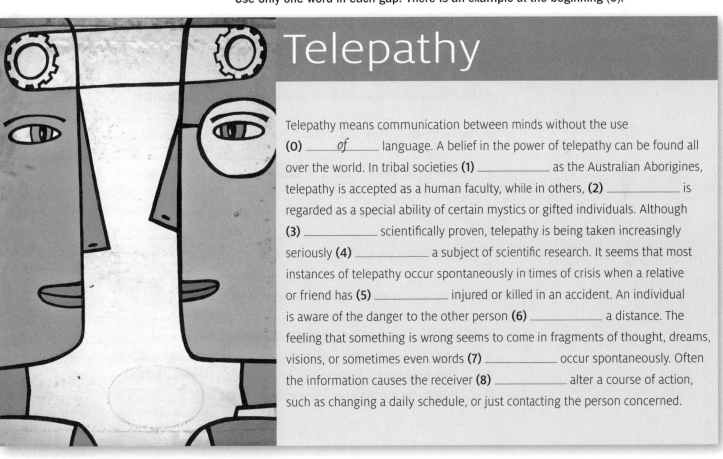

# Telepathy

Telepathy means communication between minds without the use **(0)** __of__ language. A belief in the power of telepathy can be found all over the world. In tribal societies **(1)** _____ as the Australian Aborigines, telepathy is accepted as a human faculty, while in others, **(2)** _____ is regarded as a special ability of certain mystics or gifted individuals. Although **(3)** _____ scientifically proven, telepathy is being taken increasingly seriously **(4)** _____ a subject of scientific research. It seems that most instances of telepathy occur spontaneously in times of crisis when a relative or friend has **(5)** _____ injured or killed in an accident. An individual is aware of the danger to the other person **(6)** _____ a distance. The feeling that something is wrong seems to come in fragments of thought, dreams, visions, or sometimes even words **(7)** _____ occur spontaneously. Often the information causes the receiver **(8)** _____ alter a course of action, such as changing a daily schedule, or just contacting the person concerned.

# Grammar

**Conditionals**

**1** Complete these conditional sentences using the correct form of the verb in brackets.

**a** If we're home early tonight, we _____ (go) swimming with you.

**b** If Paul drinks coffee at night, it _____ (take) him ages to get to sleep.

**c** If Anna hung her clothes up, her room _____ (not look) so untidy.

**d** If I see your father in the next hour, I _____ (tell) him you're looking for him.

**e** If Andrew hadn't been so rude, his colleagues _____ (not stop) talking to him.

**f** My mother never gives people lifts in her car if she _____ (be) on her own.

**g** The car seat _____ (not get) wet if you had closed the window.

**h** My grandfather can't see very well if he _____ (not have got) his glasses on.

**i** I _____ (phone) you if I can't get there.

**j** You'd be better at tennis if you _____ (practise) more regularly.

**2** Rewrite these sentences as Type 2 or 3 conditional sentences.

**EXAMPLE**

*He's tired because he works all the time.*
*If he didn't work all the time, he wouldn't be tired.*

**a** Sue was ill, so she didn't go to the party.

_____

**b** I don't often go to the theatre because there isn't one in my town.

_____

**c** Jeff couldn't play football because he'd broken his leg.

_____

**d** My mother never goes swimming because she's afraid of water.

_____

**e** I'd like to buy a yacht, but I haven't got £100,000 to spare.

_____

**f** It didn't snow, so we couldn't go skiing.

_____

**g** I can't send her a postcard because I don't know her address.

_____

**h** He walked into the road sign because he wasn't looking where he was going.

_____

**3** Choose the correct word or phrase in these sentences.

**a** You'll be late *unless / provided that* you leave now.

**b** I'll give you a lift in my car *as long as / unless* you don't smoke.

**c** *If / Unless* you don't stop eating, you're going to make yourself ill.

**d** I'm sure we'll have a good holiday, *provided that / unless* the weather's good.

**e** *If / Unless* you tell me what's wrong, I can't help you.

# Writing Part 2 – Article

1 **The following first sentences A–D and second sentences 1–4 have been taken from articles on aspects of communication. Match the second sentences with the opening sentences they follow.**

**Opening sentences**

A It is essential to establish good lines of communication in order to achieve productive working relationships within companies and other large organizations.

B The ability to use and understand a common language is an essential aspect of getting to know other people and of forming relationships with them.

C In almost every aspect of human life, success depends on effective communication.

D Effective communication between doctors, nurses and their patients is an essential feature of high-quality medical care.

**Second sentences**

1 A simple example of this would be the way in which, as parents, we establish close connections with our children by talking and listening to them.

2 Ineffective communication, or a breakdown in communication, can have serious effects, including a wrong diagnosis or even incorrect treatment.

3 Research has shown clearly that employers who invest time and effort in internal communications are more likely to be trusted by their employees.

4 For example, in the workplace poor communication can lead to misunderstandings and the setting up of emotional barriers.

2 **Match these third sentences e–h with the first and second sentences above.**

e This in turn can result in further problems, especially if employees start to question the ability of their managers and colleagues.

f By contrast, poor lines of communication in organizations will almost inevitably result in lack of motivation in staff.

g Patients with a poor understanding of the language spoken by their doctor or nurse may need help from another person who knows both languages.

h Another clear example is the way in which teachers use language to educate children.

## Listening Part 3

1 🔊 1.12 **You will hear five short extracts in which people are talking about juvenile crime. For questions 1–5, choose from the list (A–H) what each speaker says. Use the letters only once. There are three extra letters which you do not need to use.**

A  Vandals should be punished.

B  Parents are responsible if their children break the law.

C  I sympathize with young people.

D  Fear of crime affects people's lives.

E  I blame the society we live in today.

F  Young people don't respect anyone.

G  Parents can't always control their children.

H  Pressure from others is often to blame.

Speaker 1  **1** ☐
Speaker 2  **2** ☐
Speaker 3  **3** ☐
Speaker 4  **4** ☐
Speaker 5  **5** ☐

## Reading and Use of English Part 7

1 **You are going to read an article on page 71 about shoplifting. For questions 1–10, choose from the sections (A–E). The sections may be chosen more than once.**

**Which paragraph**

states that shoplifters feel they are treated wrongly?  **1** ☐

explains how some people make a career out of shoplifting?  **2** ☐

gives the writer's opinion about what should be done about the situation?  **3** ☐

says that many shoplifters worry about being arrested?  **4** ☐

suggests that all kinds of people can be shoplifters?  **5** ☐

gives the most common reason why people consistently shoplift?  **6** ☐

states that peer pressure often causes some people to shoplift?  **7** ☐

states the writer's assumption that the reader will agree with his view?  **8** ☐

says that some shoplifters believe their actions are justified?  **9** ☐

describes a point of view which is different from the writer's?  **10** ☐

# Why Do Shoplifters Steal?

**Peter Berlin, founder of NASP (the National Association for Shoplifting Prevention), explains why.**

### A

1 Basically, there are two types of shoplifters. The first group consists of addicts, who steal to buy drugs, and hardened criminals, who steal for resale and profit as a lifestyle. The second is made up of non-professional shoplifters. 5 These make up the majority, and they steal for a variety of reasons, mostly related to common life situations and their personal ability (or inability) to cope. These individuals know right from wrong, they know there are consequences and they often have the money to pay, but they continue 10 to steal anyway. Few of us would deny that we like to get things for free, but most people don't cross the line and steal the item, so why do they?

### B

The answer is – to most non-professional shoplifters – that 'getting something for nothing' is like giving themselves a 15 'reward'. A study found that shopping was second only to eating as the primary way people reward themselves. Take it one step further and you can easily see how 'shoplifting' the merchandise increases the reward. Shoplifting also gives them a 'high', which many will tell you is the 20 'true reward' rather than the merchandise itself. This adrenaline rush temporarily eliminates their feelings of anger, frustration, depression or other unhappiness in their lives. And, realizing how easy it is to get this 'high', they are pulled towards doing it again and again. Even though 25 most non-professional shoplifters feel guilty, ashamed or remorseful about what they do, and are afraid of getting caught, the pull is too strong to resist.

### C

Not all shoplifters steal because of some unhappiness in their lives, however. For some, it's a 'substitute for loss' 30 (a divorce, the loss of a job or a loved one, for example). For others, it's 'payback' for all they feel they give to others and how little they get back in return. The reasons why juveniles shoplift vary slightly from adults. Sometimes it is because they are depressed, confused or bored. But most 35 commonly, it is because they want nice things which they can't afford, are encouraged to by friends, or simply want to see if they can get away with it. Sometimes, they are just mad at the world and want to strike back.

### D

Of course, some people don't see shoplifting as a 40 functional or psychological problem. They say, 'What do you mean that a person can't stop shoplifting? Of course they can, they're just greedy.' The idea that shoplifting is an addiction is ridiculous, they say. 'People who shoplift should go to jail, not be treated gently or told they have 45 an addiction. This is like telling them it's okay to steal because they really can't help it.' The irony is that most shoplifters who have developed a habit or addiction believe they should be punished when caught. What offenders often resent, however, is being simply thrown into jail with 50 hardened criminals and not being given the help or support they need to help prevent them from repeating the offence.

### E

In summary, for millions of people shoplifting is simply another inappropriate way of coping with pressure and stress – similar to overeating, drinking, taking drugs or 55 gambling. It is not an issue of good vs bad people, rich vs poor, young vs old or education vs illiteracy. At any time in a person's life, the temptation to 'get something for nothing' and the desire to reward oneself can easily be present. Raising public awareness about the problem and 60 delivering needed programmes and services to people who shoplift will reduce the number of people who become involved, and improve the quality of life for everyone.

unit 12   society

# Vocabulary

## Crime vocabulary

1 Put the letters in *italics* in the correct order to make words related to crime. The first letter is in bold.

a She was *errste**a**d* by a store detective as she was leaving the shop and accused of *flipginto**s**h*.

b Some people don't consider *rag**b**urly* a serious crime. But once you've been *reg**b**uld*, you never feel entirely safe in your own home.

c He was charged with *deep**s**ing* – hc had been doing sixty in a thirty limit – and *krin**d**-gindvir*.

d People who get into fights at football matches are not fans, they are *loogina**h**s*.

e The *gu**m**reg* pushed the woman to the ground and ran off with her handbag.

f Some people think that painting graffiti is an act of *mailsda**n**v* comparable to smashing up phone boxes.

2 Complete sentences a–d with appropriate words from this list, making any necessary changes. Some words are used more than once.

| | | | | |
|---|---|---|---|---|
| arrest | bail | charge | commit | court |
| death penalty | guilty | judge | jury | probation |
| sentence | trial | verdict | | |

a In England and Wales, when someone who is suspected of ＿＿＿＿＿＿ a crime is caught, they are ＿＿＿＿＿＿ by police officers, taken to a police station, and held in custody. After questioning, if the police believe the person is guilty of the crime, they will be formally ＿＿＿＿＿＿ .

b The person usually appears in ＿＿＿＿＿＿ the next day to confirm their name and address. The magistrate then decides whether to release them on ＿＿＿＿＿＿ . This is a sum of money that someone agrees to pay if the person accused of the crime does not show up at their ＿＿＿＿＿＿ . If the magistrate refuses to grant bail, the person has to stay in prison until the day of their ＿＿＿＿＿＿ .

c The trial date is usually set several months ahead. If the crime is serious, then the evidence will be heard by a ＿＿＿＿＿＿ made up of twelve men and women. After they have heard all the evidence, they will give their ＿＿＿＿＿＿ . The person is found ＿＿＿＿＿＿ or not ＿＿＿＿＿＿ .

d The ＿＿＿＿＿＿ is the most important person in the court room. He or she will decide on the punishment. This could range from ＿＿＿＿＿＿ , where someone who has ＿＿＿＿＿＿ a minor crime is not sent to prison if they behave well over a period of time, to a life-＿＿＿＿＿＿ for the most serious crimes. The ＿＿＿＿＿＿ for murder was abolished in Great Britain in 1965. However, it still exists in many US states and other countries around the world.

## ➕ Phrasal verbs with *up*

3 Complete these sentences with the correct form of one of these verbs and *up*.

| | | | | | | |
|---|---|---|---|---|---|---|
| clear | drink | eat | fill | tear | tidy | wrap |

a The boy threw a carrier bag at the shopkeeper and ordered her to ＿＿＿＿＿＿ it ＿＿＿＿＿＿ .

b I was so angry that I ＿＿＿＿＿＿ the letter ＿＿＿＿＿＿ into small pieces.

c She ＿＿＿＿＿＿ the present in pretty gold paper.

d 'If you ＿＿＿＿＿＿ all your milk, you can have a bar of chocolate,' the woman said to her son.

e My desk is in such a mess. I suppose I'd better ＿＿＿＿＿＿ it ＿＿＿＿＿＿ .

f ＿＿＿＿＿＿ , everyone! Don't let the food get cold.

g It took us three hours to ＿＿＿＿＿＿ the mess after the party.

# Reading and Use of English Part 3

**1** For questions 1–8, read the text below. Use the word given in capitals at the end of some of the lines to form a word that fits in the gap in the same line. There is an example at the beginning (0).

## Our throwaway society

| | |
|---|---|
| Our society today is based on consumerism. While (**0**) *environmentalists* campaign | **ENVIRONMENT** |
| for us to 'reduce, recycle and re-use', we have adopted 'replace' as our ideology. | |
| Whether it is large items like (**1**) _____ goods and cars or smaller things | **HOUSE** |
| like (**2**) _____ nappies and tissues, we are constantly replacing things | **DISPOSE** |
| with little regard for the environment or our own (**3**) _____ situation. In our | **FINANCE** |
| desire to keep up with our neighbours, friends and colleagues, we have to own the | |
| very latest (**4**) _____ and gadgets. Once we have acquired these, we feel a | **EQUIP** |
| sense of pleasure and (**5**) _____ until a new model on the market makes | **ACHIEVE** |
| our (**6**) _____ outdated. Then there is a rush to dispose of these | **POSSESS** |
| (**7**) _____ items and to replace them with the most up-to-date models. It no | **WANT** |
| longer matters if the items are still perfectly (**8**) _____ ; what matters is | **FUNCTION** |
| that there is a new model available which we simply have to have. | |

# Writing Part 1

**1** Rewrite each pair of sentences as one sentence using the words in brackets.

   **a** Older people are scared to go into the town centre at night. Many young people are too. (both … and)

   _____

   **b** The bars and clubs are open until late. Some people end up drinking too much. (as)

   _____

   **c** Some people become argumentative. They get into fights. (as well as)

   _____

   **d** The number of police officers on the street should be increased. More CCTV cameras should be installed and linked directly to the police station. (in addition to)

   _____

   **e** Buses should run throughout the night. Then people wouldn't have to walk home. (so that)

   _____

   **f** These improvements would make our town a safer place to be at night. They would make it a more pleasant place to be at night. (not only … but also)

   _____

# Grammar

## Probability and possibility

**1** Use a modal verb from the list in an appropriate tense to rephrase the parts of the sentences in *italics*. There may be more than one possible answer. The first one is done as an example.

| can't | could | might | must |
|-------|-------|-------|------|

**EXAMPLE**

Wife    Was the meal all right? Heather and Dave didn't eat much.

Husband    It was very nice. *Maybe they weren't hungry.*
<u>They might not have been hungry.</u>

**a** Sally    Well, I *suppose it is possible that I* misheard the name.

**b**    Janis said she'd be here by one if she managed to get away. It's quarter past now, so *I'm sure she isn't* coming.

**c** Susie    Is Alan coming to the party?

Julie    *Maybe I'll* invite him. I haven't made up my mind yet.

**d** Fran    Oh no! This isn't my suitcase!

Julian    Then you *took* the wrong one by mistake. Is there a name anywhere?

**e** Angie    Maria tried out that cheese soufflé recipe you gave her when we were round on Saturday, but it was a disaster. It didn't rise.

Nicky    The oven *probably wasn't* hot enough.

**f** Lynne    Which one's Emma's new boyfriend?

Liz    *It's probably* that tall guy over there with the long hair. He's the only one that looks like a musician.

**g**    I don't think that's William's jacket, but *maybe I'm* wrong.

**h** Man    Waiter, this bill is for £100. We only had coffee and sandwiches. *I'm sure you've* made a mistake.

**i** Peter    We should be there by now. We've been driving for forty minutes. Val said it would only take us twenty minutes after the crossroads.

Rob    Well, *we've obviously* taken a wrong turning somewhere.

**j** Alison    James said he had transferred the money into my account, but it still isn't there.

Will    *Maybe you didn't give* him the right account number. Have you checked?

**k** Josh    Where's Jane? She said she was coming.

Tom    *Maybe she's* coming later.

**l** Jill    Denise was looking very fed up after the maths exam.

Chris    She always gets top marks in maths, though. *Maybe it's* something else that's bothering her.

**2** Choose the correct answer in *italics* in these sentences.

**a** Joe and Liz *can't / mustn't* have gone on holiday. Dave says he saw them yesterday.

**b** Andrew *mustn't / can't* be tired. He wants to play another round of golf.

**c** Diana *may / can* be coming later.

**d** She *can't / mustn't* have meant to upset you.

**e** You *can / could* be right, I suppose.

## Articles

**3** Complete the gaps in these sentences with *a / an*, *the* or Ø if no article is required.

**a** He was born in the United States, but he emigrated to _____ West Indies when he was still a young man.

**b** _____ new hostel for _____ homeless is being built in _____ town centre.

**c** _____ meal was great. Thanks for inviting me.

**d** Joyce works as _____ nurse. Her husband is _____ architect. Both their sons are _____ lawyers.

**e** 'They've just bought _____ villa by _____ sea.'
'How many rooms has _____ villa got? Has it got _____ swimming pool?'

**f** Can I have _____ glass of water and _____ cheese sandwich, please?

**g** 'Have you been on _____ holiday yet?'
'No, _____ holiday we had booked was cancelled at _____ last minute.'

**h** _____ highest mountain in _____ world is _____ Mount Everest. It's in _____ Himalayas.

**4** Complete the gaps in these common English sayings with *a / an, the* or Ø if no article is required. Then match them with their meanings 1–10.

**a** There's no such thing as _____ free lunch.

**b** _____ pen is mightier than _____ sword.

**c** No man is _____ island.

**d** _____ people who live in _____ glass houses shouldn't throw _____ stones.

**e** You can't make _____ omelette without breaking _____ few eggs.

**f** _____ beggars can't be _____ choosers.

**g** _____ actions speak louder than _____ words.

**h** _____ beauty is in _____ eye of the beholder.

**i** Don't judge _____ book by its cover.

**j** You can lead _____ horse to _____ water, but you can't make it drink.

**1** It's impossible to live without other people. We all need the help of others at some time.

**2** People all have different ideas about what is beautiful.

**3** You can't achieve something important without some downsides.

**4** You can give someone the opportunity to do something, but you can't force them to do it if they don't want to.

**5** You can't form an opinion of someone or something by appearance alone.

**6** It's not possible to get something for nothing. Everything comes at a cost.

**7** What a person actually does means more than what they say they will do.

**8** You shouldn't criticize others for something you are guilty of yourself.

**9** When there's no choice available, you have to be satisfied with what you get.

**10** People who write books, poems, etc. have a greater effect on history and human affairs than soldiers and wars.

# Vocabulary

## ➕ Phrasal verbs with *get*

**1** Read the meanings of these phrasal verbs with *get*. Then complete the sentences below with the correct form of one of the verbs, making any necessary changes.

*get away* – have a holiday

*get away with* – escape without being caught or punished

*get by* – to manage to live / survive with few resources

*get down* – depress

*get on* – (1) make progress; (2) have a friendly relationship with someone

*get out* – escape from a place

*get over* – recover from a shock or illness

**a** 'She _____ it for so long because no one suspected a little old lady would steal,' said a police spokesperson.

**b** Mary Lou asked me how Neville _____ at school.

**c** Eric _____ with his brother when they were young, but they're good friends now.

**d** Even if you haven't got time for a proper break, try and _____ for a few days.

**e** I hate winter – the cold weather and short days really _____ me _____ .

**f** When we were in Thailand, we _____ with sign-language and the half dozen words of Thai that we knew.

**g** Keith still can't _____ winning so much money.

**h** The prisoner _____ by climbing over the high wall that surrounds the jail.

# Key

## Unit 1

### Listening page 4

1 C   2 A   3 B   4 C   5 B   6 A
7 C   8 A

### Audio script

**1**

**Woman** Is that really you?

**Man** It certainly is.

**Woman** You look so young.

**Man** It was taken nearly five years ago.

**Woman** I don't think I'd recognize you from this.

**Man** I know what you mean. When I arrived yesterday, *the border officer gave me a very strange look.* I could tell he was wondering if it was really me.

**Woman** What happened?

**Man** Well, he started by asking me questions, like where had I been, *what flight I'd arrived on* and what the purpose of my visit was. Then he spoke to a colleague – I could see they were talking about me. They kept looking up and then down at the photo again. It was a bit worrying.

**2**

**Woman** Hi, just thought I'd give you a quick ring to say *I'll be arriving at the station at 10.30 tomorrow morning.* If you can come to the station to pick me up, I'll wait near the main entrance with my suitcase. If you can't, don't worry, I can easily get a taxi – I know your address. I'll probably be wearing a bright red jacket and jeans. If it's sunny, I'll have my sunglasses on – but you should still recognize me. I'm really looking forward to meeting you. Bye.

**3**

**Man** Well, obviously you need to be able to run fast. But over a fairly short distance. You don't need to be able to run a hundred metres, for example. A lot of us start off as sprinters and then change over because we're not quite suited to it. Speed is crucial because, as a rule, the speed you achieve just before take-off determines your height, and *it's that which determines the distance you jump.* Obviously other factors come into play, too, like the speed of the wind behind you …

**4**

**Footballer** I'll be out for at least two months because of the injury. Obviously I was a bit concerned at first, but the doctors say it's a clean break and don't expect any complications, which is a relief.

**Reporter** It was a hard tackle, though.

**Footballer** Yes, and I know some people would have been absolutely furious if it had happened to them, but football's a hard game. These things happen.

**Reporter** Of course it means you'll miss playing in the cup final next Saturday. It would have been your first cup final, wouldn't it?

**Footballer** *Yes, and it goes without saying that I'm extremely upset that I won't be playing.*

**5**

**Man** *If you forget your lines, don't worry. I'll be standing at the side of the stage, and I'll prompt you if that happens.* Remember to speak in a nice loud voice, too, so that everyone at the back can hear you. Two other very important things: no chewing gum, please. And whatever you do, don't wave to your parents. That's all. Any questions? No? Fine, then you can all go and get into your costumes. Good luck, everyone, I'm sure you'll be brilliant!

**6**

**Woman** I think to be successful these days you have to appeal to a wide audience – both men and women. You have to be a bit different to everyone else, and you have to come across well on television. All of these are true as far as Frank Smith is concerned, but I think the main reason he has been more successful than some of the other comedians around is because *he can do other things as well. He's not just a comedian. He makes a good chat show host, and he's not a bad singer either. In fact, you could say he's an all-round performer.*

**7**

**Woman** At the moment I'm doing everything. I take the kids to school, pick them up, make their tea, take Jack to his judo class, take Anna to her ballet class. I'm not complaining, because I know you're just as busy as me, but it would be a great help if you could sort out their Saturday activities at least – take Jack to his football practice and Anna to her riding lessons. *It's just so tiring organizing everything all of the time, and it would be nice if you could do your share.*

**8**

**Man** Now the first time you try to do this, it's quite difficult; but like everything else, practice makes perfect. It helps if you've got quite a bit of space around you, and don't try it in a kitchen with a low ceiling. When you're ready, stand with your feet apart, and *hold the frying pan at arm's length. Then, flick your wrist with an upward movement as hard as you can, and be ready to catch it when it comes down,* which it will unless you've thrown it too high and it's got stuck to the ceiling. If that happens, try again.

## Vocabulary page 4

1 a doing     e doing
   b make     f 've made / made
   c do     g make
   d to do / doing

## Grammar page 5

1 a must / should
   b have to / need to
   c must
   d had to
   e must / need to / should
   f need to

2 a don't have to
   b needn't
   c didn't need to show
   d don't have to / don't need to
   e didn't have to

3 a compulsory     d is allowed
   b forbidden     e don't have to
   c can't

4 When you're twelve, you can / you're allowed to buy pets.
You can't / you're not allowed to buy pets until you're twelve.

When you're thirteen, you can / you're allowed to get a part-time job.
You can't / you're not allowed to get a part-time job until you're thirteen.

When you're sixteen, you can / you're allowed to leave school.
You can't / you're not allowed to leave school until you're sixteen.

When you're eighteen, you can / you're allowed to buy cigarettes.
You can't / you're not allowed to buy cigarettes until you're eighteen.

When you're eighteen, you can / you're allowed to vote in elections.
You can't / you're not allowed to vote in elections until you're eighteen.

When you're sixteen, you can / you're allowed to become a soldier.
You can't / you're not allowed to become a soldier until you're sixteen.

When you're seventeen, you can / you're allowed to drive a car.
You can't / you're not allowed to drive a car until you're seventeen.

## Reading and Use of English

### page 6

1 D    2 B    3 A    4 B    5 C    6 D

## Grammar page 7

1 a I'm driving
   b You're always telling
   c belongs
   d I work, I'm travelling
   e I don't usually eat, tastes
   f is expecting

2 a shines     h are visiting
   b seems     i knows
   c speak     j looks
   d am trying     k get
   e know     l leave / are leaving
   f am making     m arrive / arriving
   g am spending

## Writing page 8

4 It is clear that for some of these people, such experiments with appearance are successful, (a) **but** things can go seriously wrong. Unfortunately, (b) **this** can cause great unhappiness and can even ruin people's lives.

3 It seems that the majority of operations are on people (c) **who** are simply unhappy with the way they look. They believe that altering their physical appearance will increase their confidence or make them more attractive to other people. They hope surgery will make it easier for them to make friends or to get a good job.

1 (d) **There** have been many recent reports about cosmetic surgery operations that have gone wrong. When I heard about these, I wondered why so many people choose to have these operations.

5 (e) **To** conclude, I would suggest that everyone considering cosmetic surgery should first receive honest medical advice and be warned about the risks involved.

2 (f) **There** is no doubt that some cosmetic operations are necessary for medical or psychological reasons, (g) **for** example for patients who have been involved in serious accidents. (h) **However**, it is clear from the number of operations conducted every year that most 'patients' are not in (i) **this** category.

## Reading and Use of English

### page 8

1 A    2 B    3 D    4 D    5 A    6 C
7 C    8 A

## Vocabulary page 9

1

| | | | | | | | | |
|---|---|---|---|---|---|---|---|---|
| **1** | | S | T | A | R | E | | |
| **2** | | T | O | E | | | | |
| **3** | N | O | T | I | C | E | | |
| **4** | P | A | L | M | | | | |
| **5** | | G | A | Z | E | | | |
| **6** | | C | R | A | W | L | | |
| **7** | S | H | O | U | L | D | E | R | S |

3 a flat     d wide
   b freely     e lately
   c rough

4 a finger     e arm
   b back     f head
   c tongue     g neck
   d feet     h hair

# Unit 2

## Reading and Use of English

### page 10

1 B    2 D    3 C    4 A    5 B    6 A
7 B    8 A    9 D    10 C

## Vocabulary page 11

1 a undervalued
   b overdressed, underdressed
   c overgrown
   d extra-curricular
   e overcritical / hypercritical
   f extraordinary
   g overqualified

2 a A cat which got into the house through an open window set off the burglar alarm / set the burglar alarm off.
   b We'd better set off early tomorrow. We've got a long way to travel.
   c Recently more and more people have been setting up their own internet companies.
   d The police set their dogs on the bank robbers as they tried to escape.
   e The terrible rain storms we've had recently have set back the house-building programme / set the house-building programme back by several months.
   f I'm going to write to the principal setting out my ideas / setting my ideas out for improvements to the school.

## Grammar page 12

1
a have you been able to
b can't
c couldn't, couldn't read
d Both are possible
e could
f Both are possible
g can't
h were able to

2
a Can you / Are you able to / Will you be able to
b Could you / Were you able to
c Will robots ever be able to
d Could we / Would we be able to
e Has David been able to
f Can you / Could you / Are you able to / Will you be able to / Would you be able to
g Could you have

3
a will be able to
b couldn't
c could
d couldn't
e were able to
f haven't been able to
g couldn't
h was able to

4
a couldn't
b managed
c couldn't have
d be able to
e hasn't been able to
f succeeded

## Reading and Use of English
page 13

1 appearance
2 independently
3 effective
4 sticky
5 belief
6 surroundings
7 endangered
8 destruction

## Vocabulary page 13

1
a take-off
b hold-up
c turnout
d takeaway
e breakout
f let-down
g breakthrough
h outbreak

## Listening page 14

1 brain damage
2 language and comprehension
3 had (any) piano lessons
4 vocabulary
5 any calculator
6 (third) shape
7 describe
8 mental stimulus
9 9-to-5
10 in an office

## Audio script

I have always been fascinated by how the human mind works, so I was delighted when I was given the opportunity to interview the autistic savant Daniel Tammet. For those of you not familiar with the term, an 'autistic savant' is a person with autism who is exceptionally gifted in a specialized field.

An estimated 10% of autistic people have 'savant' abilities, but no one knows exactly why. *What is known, however, is that savants have usually had some kind of brain damage, such as a blow to the head, and it is that damage which creates the savant.* While *many savants struggle with language and comprehension, which are primarily left-hemisphere skills*, they often have amazing skills in mathematics and memory, which are primarily right-hemisphere skills. *The blind American savant Leslie Lemke played a Tchaikovsky piano concerto after hearing it once, and he had never had any piano lessons.* And the British savant Stephen Wiltshire was able to draw a highly accurate map of the London skyline from memory after a single helicopter trip over the city.

*Typically, savants have a limited vocabulary, but not Daniel.* He speaks six languages and is even creating his own. He is also a mathematical genius and is obsessed with counting. In fact, as we talked he counted the stitches on my shirt. *Daniel doesn't actually 'calculate', however, though he can give you the answer to a maths problem faster than any calculator.* He sees numbers as shapes, colours and textures. The number five, for instance, is a clap of thunder. *When he multiplies numbers together, he sees two shapes. The image starts to change and a third shape emerges. That is the answer.* Daniel describes it as 'like maths but without having to think'.

*What makes Daniel particularly interesting to scientists is that he can describe what he does.* The others just do things but can't tell scientists how. So, he could provide the key which scientists need to understand how the mind of an autistic savant works.

However, because Daniel is autistic, he can't do many of the ordinary things the rest of us can. He can't, for example, drive a car, or even tell right from left. And although he lives just a five-minute walk from the beach, he never goes there – there are too many pebbles to count. *Trips to the supermarket, too, are always a chore. There's too much mental stimulus.* He has to look at every shape, texture, and price.

*Daniel has never been able to work 9 to 5.* It would be too difficult to fit around his daily routine. For instance, he has to drink his cups of tea at exactly the same time every day. Things have to happen in the same order: he always brushes his teeth before he has his shower. He likes to do things in his own time, and in his own way, *so working in an office with targets and bureaucracy just wouldn't work. Instead, he has set up his own business, at home, writing email courses in language learning, numeracy, and literacy for private clients. It has had the added benefit of keeping human interaction to a minimum.*

## Vocabulary page 14

1
a most superstitious
b heavier
c most expensive
d more clearly
e fatter
f more carefully
g cleverest, highest
h more clearly
i worse
j best, better

## Writing page page 14

1
a Good to hear from you
b more than happy
c To start with
d make up your mind
e fun
f free
g hard
h So
i perhaps
j for a while
k start
l suits
m till
n quite
o hope this helps
p All the best

2 a inform you, receive, to be claimed
  b Simply write, your chosen items
  c at your convenience
  d they will be reserved, notify us, to avoid additional charges
  e photographs, required documents, your identity card will be issued immediately

# Unit 3

## Vocabulary  page 16

1 a give back     d giving away
  b gave out      e gave in / gave up
  c give up

## Grammar  page 16

1 a 3   b 1   c 2
2 a never got used to
  b used to smoke
  c are used to getting dressed
  d get used to driving
  e did you use to live

## Listening  page 17

1 C   2 A   3 C   4 B   5 B   6 C   7 B

### Audio script

**Int** This evening in our series 'In my experience' our guest is Maggie Lyons, an adviser to people who are addicted to gambling. She provides support to individuals and gives talks to local community groups. Welcome, Maggie.

**Maggie** Thank you – hello.

**Int** You have not always worked as an adviser, have you?

**Maggie** No, certainly not. *I was once addicted to gambling myself.*

**Int** Can I start by asking you how you became addicted and, perhaps more importantly, how you managed to kick the habit?

**Maggie** Well, let me start by saying it was a lot more difficult to stop than it was to start. It began in a very innocent way, really. A group of us at work used to meet for a game of cards every week. *We played for very low stakes,* but for some reason I almost always won, and sadly, I got it into my head that I was a lucky person.

**Int** That does sound very innocent. How much money did you actually make?

**Maggie** Next to nothing, really – probably about five pounds a week. Playing for money just made the game a bit more exciting. Anyway, because I was convinced that I was a lucky person, I started gambling online – and strangely I went on winning. Believe it or not, in my first week, I made over a hundred pounds. Perhaps my mistake was that *I didn't tell anyone what I was doing. I kept it such a good secret.*

**Int** How much money did you make in the end?

**Maggie** In the first month, I made over two thousand pounds. The more I won, the more frequently I played, and it wasn't long before I was playing for three or four hours every day.

**Int** And did you go on winning?

**Maggie** For a while, yes. I was beginning to think I couldn't lose, so I gambled larger and larger sums of money, until one day I lost five thousand pounds.

**Int** Five thousand?

**Maggie** Yes, but even then, I thought I'd win again if I went on playing. But over the next few weeks, I lost more often than I won, until I had almost no money left in the bank.

**Int** So what did you do?

**Maggie** In the end *I asked my dad for a loan* – I told him I needed a new car.

**Int** And nobody advised you to stop?

**Maggie** No – because nobody knew. I think my close friends might have guessed but didn't know for sure. Anyway, to cut a long story short, eventually I realized gambling was ruining my life and I decided to look for help.

**Int** Where did you go?

**Maggie** I phoned a helpline and got an appointment with an addiction counsellor. She was brilliant.

**Int** How did she help?

**Maggie** She said it was the activity I was addicted to, rather than the money, *so her advice was to gradually reduce the amount of time I spent online, and to gamble smaller and smaller amounts of money each time.* At one point I thought about getting together with other addicts, but decided against it in the end.

**Int** And were you able to follow that advice?

**Maggie** Well, eventually, yes, but I can't pretend it was easy.

**Int** Did you go on losing money?

**Maggie** Sometimes I won and sometimes I lost, but the amounts were never very large, so the impact on my life was not as great as it had been. After two months I began to get bored. Almost without realizing it, *I found I was choosing to spend my money on clothes, books, going to the cinema – things like that.*

**Int** So when was the last time you gambled?

**Maggie** Three years ago. I can't believe I was so stupid.

**Int** And now you help other people with the same problem?

**Maggie** Yes, that's right. I work as a volunteer for the same organization that helped me. I use the same method, too.

**Int** And does it always work?

**Maggie** Usually, yes. The thing is, it takes people different lengths of time to kick the habit, but *in the end they nearly all do – or they at least reduce their gambling to a level they can control. Some people are happy with that.*

**Int** You must find it very rewarding.

**Maggie** I do – because I know how dreadful addiction can be.

**Int** Next, we're going to talk to someone who is still addicted to online gambling and ask Maggie to give her some advice.

## Grammar  page 17

1 a experience    e language
  b lights        f exercises
  c noise         g room
  d much time

2 a bit / piece / word
  b bit / piece / sheet
  c bit / stroke

d bit
e bit / item / piece
f box
g piece

## Reading and Use of English
page 18

1 D   2 E   3 F   4 B   5 G   6 A
Extra sentence: C

## Vocabulary page 19

1 b inspiration     g disappoint
  c relieve         h appreciation
  d explanation     i respond
  e provision       j belief
  f satisfaction

2 a huge, old, Roman
  b unusual, green, cotton
  c beautiful, tall, modern
  d large, square, black and white
  e tiny, brand new, Japanese

## Reading and Use of English
page 20

1 their          5 with
2 where          6 who / that
3 or             7 from
4 well           8 up

## Vocabulary page 20

1 Adverbs of manner: dangerously,
  deliberately, hard, sensitively
  Comment adverbs: interestingly,
  luckily, surprisingly, unfortunately
  Focusing adverbs: especially, even, only
  Frequency adverbs: always,
  occasionally, rarely, sometimes
  Adverbs of degree: absolutely,
  completely, totally, very

2 b **Occasionally** / **Sometimes** I go the
    theatre if there's something good
    on.
  c My brother was stopped by the
    police because he was driving
    **dangerously**.
  d I hate long road journeys,
    **especially** in the winter when the
    roads are icy.
  e **Luckily** / **Surprisingly**, my sister
    passed her driving test first time.
  f When I was four, I **deliberately**
    broke my brother's favourite toy /
    broke my brother's favourite toy
    **deliberately**.
  g That was a terrible fire. The house
    was **completely** / **totally** destroyed.

## Writing page 21

2 E, h   3 C, g   4 D, c   5 H, b
6 G, a   7 F, f   8 B, d

# Unit 4

## Listening page 22

1 D   2 H   3 A   4 F   5 C
Extra letters: B, E, G

### Audio script

#### Speaker 1
My brother's three years older than me
and I think of him as my best friend.
It's funny 'cos if you'd asked any of
our relatives when we were younger
if we'd ever be this close, they'd just
have laughed. Chris and I were always
fighting. *Then when he was about
sixteen, he started having a rough time
at school – the teachers were picking on
him. At the same time I started having
arguments with Mum and Dad. Anyway,
me and Chris started talking and asking
each other for advice. It was then that we
realized we had loads in common, and
we've been friends ever since.*

#### Speaker 2
My brother's called Peter, and we've
always got on really well. We'd have the
odd argument about what to watch on TV,
stuff like that, but never anything serious.
We're pretty close in age – he was a year
ahead of me at school. When I started
school, he sort of looked after me. *I'd go
and find him at break time and tell all my
friends how fantastic it was having a big
brother.* I really missed him when he went
to university last year. He comes home
for the holidays, but it's not the same as
having him at home all the time.

#### Speaker 3
I don't see my brother much these days
– he's living in Australia. But I know he's
at the end of the phone if I need him.
We don't have much in common, but I
like to keep in touch with him. We talk
or email most weeks. We didn't get on
very well when we were younger – I was
always jealous of him. He seemed to be
able to get away with anything. *When he
was in his teens he could stay out much
later than I could.* Parents are always
stricter with their daughters, aren't they?
*I always had to tell my parents where
I was going and who with. They never
asked him anything.*

#### Speaker 4
It's sad, really, but I've never actually
liked my brother. Right from when I was
a toddler, he bullied me. I remember him
saying things like: 'We don't need you in
our family.' And he was always getting
me into trouble with Mum and Dad. If
ever I did anything wrong, he'd tell them;
he always made it sound worse than it
actually was and they always believed him.
*These days I'm just not interested in
seeing him.* We don't live in the same
place any more, so we occasionally meet
at family get-togethers, but that's about
all. We chat politely, but we haven't
really got anything to say to each other.

#### Speaker 5
*I was always the favourite.* I was bright
and extrovert – a real goody-goody.
My older brother Alex was a bit of a
tearaway. I always did better at school,
and my parents held me up as a shining
example for him to follow whenever he
was breaking windows with his football,
or refusing to do his homework. Not
surprisingly, he absolutely hated me,
and you can't really blame him. The
funny thing is, now we're grown up, no
one in the family seems to remember
this – except me, of course. We're in our
twenties now, and we get on okay, but
sometimes *I still feel guilty about being
Mum and Dad's favourite.*

## Vocabulary page 22

1 a picked us up      d picks at
  b picks on          e pick out
  c picked it up      f picked up

2 a takes             d take
  b have              e have
  c taking            f don't have

## Grammar page 23

1 a I'm going to learn
  b I'm meeting
  c I'll be walking
  d It's going to snow
  e leaves
  f I'm going to travel
  g I'll go
  h I'll have been living
  i will go up
  j lands

2 b I'm going to give up smoking
  c I'll answer it
  d ✓
  e we will have finished

f ✓
g will object
h are you going to do / will you do

3 a is going to be / will be
b am going to faint
c am going
d leaves
e will have worked / will have been working
f will turn
g am going to give up
h will be thinking

## Reading and Use of English
page 24

1 C   2 B   3 D   4 B   5 D   6 A

## Grammar   page 25

1 a too, enough     c too
  b too              d enough

2 b You aren't old enough to learn to drive.
  c You're walking too slowly to keep up with me.
  d These new jeans aren't big enough for me.
  e My brother lives too far away to come for the weekend.
  f I'm too short to reach the top shelf.
  g I'm not well enough to come on holiday with you.

## Reading and Use of English
page 26

1 didn't have (enough) time
2 is bound to pass
3 have arranged a meeting / have arranged to meet
4 has been brought in
5 are unlikely ever to go / to ever go
6 picked it up while / by / when / whilst

## Vocabulary   page 26

1 b energetic       h fair
  c creative        i organized
  d patient         j fit
  e caring          k enthusiastic
  f brave           l hard-working
  g sociable        m cheerful

## Writing   page 27

1 1 b   2 f   3 a   4 d
2 a 4   b 1   c 5   d 3   e 6   f 2

# Unit 5

## Vocabulary   page 28

1 a trip           e crossing
  b tour           f cruise
  c journey        g voyage
  d excursion

2 a did
  b campsite, put up
  c landed
  d boarded, crew, fasten
  e package
  f miss
  g coach, booked
  h ports, disembarked
  i take
  j lanes
  k souvenir

3 a pick me up      e took off
  b set off         f stop over
  c checked in      g drop you off
  d see him off

4 a seat            d time
  b tyre            e parts
  c room            f change

## Listening   page 29

1 E   2 C   3 A   4 H   5 D
Extra sentences: B, F, G

**Audio script**

**Speaker 1**
Last year, I went to France on a day trip with some friends. They were taking their car and asked if I wanted to come along as they had a spare seat. I was quite excited because I'd never travelled to France through the Channel Tunnel before – I'd always gone on the ferry – and I have to say it was much faster and much more convenient, but *it was also quite boring*. It was like being on a plane with no windows, because there was nothing to see except the car in front and the car behind. I'm not saying I wouldn't use the Tunnel again, but it certainly wasn't what I expected.

**Speaker 2**
One summer, when I was a student, I travelled round Spain by train. I went with a friend and we travelled at night to save money on accommodation. We slept in 'literas', which are bunk beds. There were six in each compartment: three on each side, one on top of the other. *The temperature in our compartment was never right – it was either boiling hot or freezing cold – and the beds were narrow and really hard. I woke up with backache every morning. If you were really unlucky, you'd be sharing with someone who snored or be woken up in the middle of the night by a ticket inspector.* It wasn't the most restful way to travel.

**Speaker 3**
The worst travelling experience I've ever had was when I was in the States. *I was flying from Newark to Washington Dulles – about an hour's flight.* We set off late, and then when we were half-way to Washington, we were told that we couldn't land because of bad weather and we had to turn back. Then, when we got back to Newark, we found that all the flights to Washington had been cancelled! *We ended up sleeping on the floor of the departure lounge! We had to complain repeatedly to the ground staff, but eventually they put us on buses to take us to our destination.*

**Speaker 4**
I don't suppose I could really recommend hitchhiking as a way of travelling these days, but when I did it, it was a common way of getting around on a tight budget. No one gave a second thought as to whether it was safe or not. When I was in my early twenties, I hitchhiked all round Europe, and never once felt in any sort of danger. I loved it. *You never got bored because every day was different – you never knew where you were going to end up, and every person who gave you a lift was different.* You might be picked up by a couple in an expensive car one day and a farmer driving a tractor the next.

**Speaker 5**
I went to China last year with a tour company. I'm not a great fan of organized holidays as a rule, but if you're going to a country where you don't know the language, and you want to see as much of it as you can in a short time, then it's a good way to do it. Our guide was very informative, and we saw an awful lot, including how people live, which was fascinating. But we didn't stop from seven in the morning till seven at night! *It was a very tiring schedule and it involved so much travelling! I'd have liked to spend a week at a beach resort at the end to recover.* But that's my only criticism.

key

## Grammar page 30

1 a went, got
  b Haven't you finished, have been doing, have done
  c got, wrote down
  d had just put, rang, thought, rushed, had stopped, reached
  e have forgotten
  f had, was wearing, had driven off
  g had just covered, went
  h was thinking, had just picked up, started
  i have been peeling
  j was sitting, had left

2 1 was driving
  2 was raining
  3 was beginning
  4 saw
  5 opened
  6 asked
  7 got in
  8 was making
  9 Had you been waiting
  10 shook
  11 tried
  12 gave
  13 noticed
  14 realized
  15 got out
  16 drove off
  17 reached
  18 had left
  19 picked it up
  20 had had

## Reading and Use of English
page 31

1 1 D   2 B   3 C   4 C   5 D   6 A
  7 A   8 B

## Reading and Use of English
page 32

1 F   2 C   3 G   4 B   5 A   6 E
Extra sentence: D

## Vocabulary page 33

1

```
F N E C D E T J I H O P S A
R A X U E P V Q M F U U E D
E I H I L A R I O U S G G F
E F A B I D R U N R I L E F
Z G U T C B O I L I N G W I
I K S B I C X Z F O H I P L
N L T P O I Y R D U A D T T
G J E P U K N E T S U I O H
S E D I S T S B M T I N Y Y
```

2 b success, unsuccessful
  c honesty, dishonest
  d maturity, immature
  e patience, impatient
  f responsibility, irresponsible

## Writing page 33

1 a enjoyable, sunny
  b kind, delicious
  c disastrous, serious
  d pretty
  e accomplished
  f useful
  g well-behaved, naughty

# Unit 6
## Reading and Use of English
page 34

1 E   2 A   3 F   4 G   5 B   6 C
Extra sentence: D

## Vocabulary page 35

1 embarrassment, boredom, annoyance, exhaustion, disappointment, amusement, frustration, surprise

2 a embarrassing
  b boring
  c annoyed
  d embarrassed
  e frustrated
  f exhausting
  g amusing
  h disappointed
  i embarrassing
  j exhausted

## Grammar page 36

1 a on coming
  b at speaking
  c of / with doing
  d at persuading
  e for breaking
  f against leaving
  g of getting
  h on passing
  i in putting up
  j at drawing, in becoming

2 a wasting, to get
  b to inform
  c to follow, to find
  d to get up, to set
  e smoking, having
  f to meet, to hear
  g being, having
  h getting

## Vocabulary page 36

1 a N   b P   c P   d P   e P   f P
  g P   h P / N   i N   j N   k N   l P

2 d in-   e un-   f im-   j un-

3 a boredom          g sense
  b optimism         h seriousness

c determination    i emotion
d efficiency       j jealousy
e friendliness     k envy
f patience         l thoughtfulness

4 a optimistic      e boredom
  b Jealousy        f Determination
  c sensible        g friendliness
  d thoughtless     h impatient

## Reading and Use of English
page 37

1 prevented me from hearing
2 went on working
3 didn't mean to insult
4 not mind if Paul comes
5 be hard to predict
6 am getting used to getting

## Vocabulary page 38

1 a serious        d close
  b strong         e hard
  c heavy          f serious

2 a soundly        f becoming
  b find           g attentively
  c hard           h passionately
  d take           i hard
  e heavily        j expressed

3
a went on / took, short
b tough / hard, make
c spent
d wide
e fierce
f break
g run, run
h severe
i breaking
j full
k paying
l rented / hired
m playing / performing
n clear / vivid

## Listening page 39

1 1 shy
  2 three seconds
  3 hole in the / a net
  4 twelve months
  5 music
  6 zoo animals
  7 rubbing
  8 feel pain
  9 a tank
  10 stimulated and interested

## Audio script

Today I'm going to talk about fish and some recent research into how their minds work. You are probably thinking 'Fish don't have minds, surely?' But that is just one of the many wrong ideas people have about fish. Today, I hope to dismiss some of these ideas. The first thing I want to say is that not all fish are the same. And I'm not talking about the obvious differences between one species of fish and another; I'm talking about differences within species. It's been known for a long time that animals like cattle and dogs are all individuals, and behave differently in different circumstances; but that's also true of fish. *Research has shown that some fish are bold individuals who are risk-takers, and others are shy and will avoid taking risks.*

Another wrong idea people have is that fish have no memory. Unfortunately, films like the Hollywood blockbuster *Finding Nemo*, which stars a forgetful blue fish called Dory, have reinforced this idea. *A fish's memory is longer than the three seconds that people credit them with.* Research has shown that they can remember experiences for many months after just a little training. *One trial involved putting fish in a big fishing net in a tank, and moving the net quickly backwards and forwards. The fish had to learn where the hole in the net was in order to get out.* It only took about five trials – that's about 15 to 20 minutes – for them to learn it. *Then when the same fish were tested 12 months later, it was found that they'd remembered exactly where the escape route was.*

There has also been some rather unusual research done on carp fairly recently. In this study they played jazz and classical music to the carp. *They trained them to perform one task if they heard jazz and a different task if they heard classical music.* You may ask how they were able to do that. Well, fish have quite a good hearing system, so they can hear the music. But whether it's the vibration of the music or the rhythm that helps them to distinguish one kind of music from the other is not yet known.

Many people ask me whether fish can feel pain. *In one recent study, when the lips of live trout were injected with bee venom, they rocked from side to side just like some zoo animals do when they're depressed or sad. They also rubbed the affected area against the sides of the tank and the gravel at the bottom. This appears to be similar to the behaviour of people and animals, who also try to reduce the intensity of pain in an affected area by rubbing it.*

However, there is another school of thought that says that *because fish don't possess a neocortex, that's the outer part of the brain believed to be responsible for consciousness, they can't feel pain* in the same way we do.

Finally, you may be wondering what my views are on keeping, for example, a goldfish as a pet. Well, that's not really for me to say, but research shows that fish are more conscious creatures than they were previously thought to be, so personally *I would be against keeping them in small glass bowls. A tank would certainly be preferable.* But put lots of things in it; change the scenery around from time to time. *If you want your fish to be happy and healthy, the most important thing is that they're stimulated and interested.*

## Writing  page 39

Music plays an important role in many people's lives. Whether it is classical music, pop music, rock music, jazz or opera, we all listen to it at one time or another for a variety of reasons.

Music can certainly affect our mood (,) but the kind of music we listen to will affect our mood differently. Upbeat music generally makes people feel happy (,) while slow music, particularly if it reminds us of a painful event in our past, can make us feel sad.

If we are feeling sad or depressed, music may lift our spirits**. H**owever, there are many other activities people can do. Many people find that doing exercise is effective. For other people, spending time with friends has the same positive effect on their mood**. B**eing out in the countryside or by the sea can also work.

To sum up, music may be a good therapy for some people when they are feeling low, but for others it can have the opposite effect**. T**here are many other activities which people can do which are equally, if not more, effective.

Note: The punctuation marks in brackets are optional.

# Unit 7

## Listening  page 40

1 B  2 A  3 A  4 B  5 C  6 A  7 C

### Audio script

**Int** Welcome to today's 'Free Time', the programme which looks at the work of unpaid volunteers. Last week, we heard from Hamid, who helps to organize a sports club for children in his neighbourhood. Today in the studio we have Jerry, a 20-year-old student. Jerry, could you start by telling us briefly what kind of volunteering you do?

**Jerry** Of course. I work on a steam railway quite near to where I study.

**Int** A steam railway – that sounds fascinating. Tell us more.

**Jerry** Well, as you've probably guessed, this is not an ordinary modern railway which takes people to and from work. It's actually a historic railway which originally opened in 1865. *It used to transport coal from the mines in the area to the nearest port*, which was about fifty kilometres away. *These days, it's mainly a tourist attraction*, although there is still a daily service which takes people from a small village to the nearest town.

**Int** And what do you do to help with the running of the railway?

**Jerry** Well, the only thing I don't do is drive the engines. That's specialist work I'm not qualified to do. But *I do everything else, from selling tickets to passengers to keeping the station tidy and serving in the café*. What I like best is helping to repair and restore old steam engines. Being an engineering student, that's not too difficult for me to do and I find it absolutely fascinating. But during the spring and summer, there are a hundred and one things to do to cater for the visitors. *So, generally speaking we do this kind of work out of the tourist season. There's a bit more time for it then.*

**Int** And how is the railway funded?

**Jerry** We get a small grant from the local council, but most of our income comes directly from visitors. *The company that owns the railway employs three full-time staff – two engine drivers and a business manager – so we need a certain amount of income just to keep the project going.* The rest of us are all volunteers.

**Int** How many of you are there?

**Jerry** It varies depending on the time of year, but we have an average of fifteen volunteers most weekends.

**Int** And what is there for visitors to do when they come to see the railway?

**Jerry** Most important of all is a journey on the train. There's ten kilometres of railway line open at the moment, and we're planning to open five more kilometres next year. Eventually, we hope to re-open the whole length of the old line as far as the port. *Some of the adult visitors remember steam trains from when they were younger – so the train journey is a real nostalgia trip for them.* And of course the kids think it's wonderful. Then there are the engine sheds where you can see old steam trains in the process of being repaired. There's a visitor centre where you can see an illustrated history of the railway. And, of course, there's the café and the gift shop, where visitors can buy postcards and souvenirs.

**Int** How much time do you manage to spend working there?

**Jerry** I get there most weekends during my summer vacation and I'm there about once a fortnight on average for the rest of the year. It's very rewarding seeing people enjoying their visit so much.

## Vocabulary page 41

1 a run out of time   d time to kill
  b save time         e waste of time
  c time off          f spare time

## Grammar page 41

1 a are employed
  b happened, was hurt
  c were / are cleaned, changed / change

  d was warned, was caught
  e were sent, broke down
  f was given
  g have been made, was taken over
  h hasn't been invited / isn't invited
  i be handed in
  j will announce / will be announcing

2 a They / We have already booked the church and sent out the invitations, so we can't cancel the wedding now.
  b You / Students must not bring food into the classroom.
  c You (will) need to feed the dog twice a day. Don't forget.
  d For a moment, Angie thought a strangely-dressed woman was following her.
  e In Britain, they / the council collect(s) people's rubbish once a week.

3 a am having / getting it delivered
  b are having their bedroom decorated
  c to have / get it repaired
  d am having / getting it cleaned
  e had it cut down
  f had it taken out
  g having / getting it cut
  h am having / getting my eyes tested
  i had it designed
  j have / get her blood pressure checked

## Reading and Use of English
page 42

1 C   2 C   3 A   4 B   5 A   6 D
7 C   8 A   9 D   10 B

## Vocabulary page 42

1 a for        f on
  b with       g by
  c of         h from
  d on         i for
  e with

2 a come out        d come up with
  b came across     e came round
  c are coming round f has come up

## Reading and Use of English
page 44

1 B   2 B   3 C   4 D   5 B   6 C
7 D   8 A

## Writing page 45

1 b 3   c 1   d 6   e 2   f 4

2 a As regards working in television, I really enjoy it.
  b In answer to your second question, I worked in the United States for three years.
  c As far as my family commitments are concerned, I am married and have one child.
  d As regards radio phone-in programmes, I have never worked on one.
  e My only question is, when does the job start?

# Unit 8

## Vocabulary page 46

1 a shop assistant
  b search engine
  c university lecturer
  d breakdown
  e keyboard
  f website
  g newsreader

2 a Maria is such a hard worker that she always gets the highest marks.
  b John's IQ is so high that he got into university when he was fourteen.
  c Claudia writes so fast that she always finishes first.
  d I know such a lot of people who wish they hadn't left school at sixteen.
  e Some people's jobs are so boring that they can't wait to retire.

## Listening page 47

1 B   2 A   3 C   4 C   5 A   6 C
7 C   8 A

**Audio script**

1

**Woman** On work days I wake up at seven o'clock to the sound of my favourite news programme. My radio alarm clock makes sure of that. I need to know what's going on in the world as soon as possible. I usually lie there with my eyes closed until I've heard the headlines and a couple of the main stories in detail. *My main interest is international stories, I suppose.*

I've listened to this programme for as long as I can remember – so long, in fact, that I now think of the main newsreaders almost as friends.

**2**

**Int** Can I ask you a few questions about the newspapers you read?

**Man** Certainly, what would you like to know?

**Int** Well first of all, do you read a newspaper every day, or only occasionally?

**Man** Every day. Actually, I read two papers – the *News Daily* on the way to work and the *Financial Times* when I get to work.

**Int** When you're reading the *News Daily*, what do you read first?

**Man** Well, *I glance at the main stories*, then turn to the back and read the day's sports news.

**3**

**Woman** I have to admit, I love those magazines that tell you all about celebrities, you know, film stars, singers, TV personalities. I love finding out the details of their private lives: who's having an affair with who, who's bought an expensive new house, who's expecting a baby. *Most of all, I like reading about what's happening in my favourite soap operas.* I know some people pretend they aren't interested in this kind of thing but I don't believe them. I think everyone's curious about how the rich and famous live their lives.

**4**

**Teenage boy** I hardly ever watch TV. I'm probably not typical of someone my age, but I find most programmes completely predictable. I get very bored watching TV – *I'd much rather be actually doing something. So, for example, I spend a fair amount of time playing football or swimming.* The only programmes I try to watch regularly are music programmes – I try to catch the charts every week. But I can honestly say, I never watch the news or documentaries. Most of all I hate game shows – they're just so middle-aged.

**5**

**Man** I'd never really thought of the internet as part of the media – but then one of my colleagues told me about all the newspapers you can get online. I subscribe to the *New York Times* – which means I get sent the online version as an email every day. It's fantastic. *I'm totally amazed that anyone still buys the paper.* You can even find out background information by following the links at the ends of the stories. It's certainly a quick and easy way of finding out what's going on in the world.

**6**

**Woman** Did you see the film on Channel 29 last night?

**Man** No, we haven't got satellite TV.

**Woman** Really? You don't know what you're missing.

**Man** *How many channels can you get?*

**Woman** *Eighty-three at the moment, but it's going up to one hundred and fifty next year.*

**Man** *I don't think I could cope with all that choice. It's bad enough at the moment, having six channels to choose from.*

**Woman** *You'd get used to it.*

**Man** *I'm not sure I'd want to get used to it – especially if greater choice meant poorer quality programmes.*

**7**

**Woman** I've recently read some research which may come as no surprise to teachers and parents of small children, but which was certainly news to me. The basic finding is this: the more often parents read to their children from a very early age, the greater the effect on their language skills, such as reading and speaking. It was found that reading to children six or seven times a week puts them almost a year ahead of those who are not read to on a regular basis. *It's clear that this will give children who are read to a massive advantage.*

**8**

**Man** What time do we need to leave in the morning?

**Woman** Half past eight at the latest.

**Man** Oh! But I've asked the decorator to come round.

**Woman** What time?

**Man** Well, I asked him to come first thing. He said he'd be here by nine. That'll be okay, won't it?

**Woman** I'm not sure. The ferry leaves at ten and it takes about an hour to get there.

**Man** Hmm – that could be a problem.

**Woman** Can't we ask him to come next week?

**Man** We could – but *I'd prefer to ring him and see if he can get here a bit earlier.*

**Woman** Well, it's worth a try.

## Vocabulary  page 48

1 a  goes by      d  going on
  b  go after      e  go up
  c  go through    f  go along with

## Reading and Use of English
page 48

1 B   2 A   3 D   4 D   5 D   6 A

## Grammar  page 50

1 a  'Hurry up. We're going to be late.'
  b  'Do you think I should wear my long dress or my short stripy one / dress?'
  c  'I think you should wear your black dress.' / 'Why don't you wear your black dress?'
  d  'I can't. It's at the dry-cleaner's.' / 'I can't because it's at the dry-cleaner's.'
  e  'I don't care what you wear, but if we're late, I might lose my job.'

2 a  Delia said (that) she'd love to and asked him what time it started. Paul replied that it started / would start (at) about ten but that she could come when she liked.
  b  Delia said (that) she'd been invited to Paul's party. Angie asked when it was.
     Delia replied that it was on Saturday. She added that she didn't want to go but (she) couldn't say no. Angie suggested that Delia should phone him / Paul on Saturday and say (that) she didn't feel well.
  c  Paul's mother warned him not to make too much noise. She added that she didn't want any complaints from the neighbours. Paul promised (that) he wouldn't.

key

d Pete asked Delia why she hadn't come to Paul's party.
Delia replied that (she hadn't gone because) everyone had said it would be boring.
Pete said (that) he'd really enjoyed it. He added that it hadn't finished till after four and (that) Angie and John had been there.

3 a John's mother told him not to speak with his mouth full.
b Laura's mother reminded her to get her father a birthday present.
c The man warned Tom not to cross the road there because it wasn't safe.
d David insisted on paying.
e Susie suggested trying the new Chinese restaurant in King Street.

## Reading and Use of English
page 51

1 up
2 enough
3 as
4 has
5 but
6 if
7 so
8 before

## Writing  page 51

1 a However
b whereas
c In fact
d On the other hand
e On the contrary
f Apart from that

2 a Local radio is a brilliant invention which / that is cheap to produce and gets large audiences.
b I can think of two advantages radio has over television, the first of which is that you can do something while you are listening. / I can think of two advantages radio has over television, the first being that you can do something while you are listening.
c There are many radio programmes about science and technology, which are, in my opinion, interesting and informative.
d We arranged to meet outside the station at 6 o'clock. I hope I can get there by then / on time.

# Unit 9

## Listening  page 52

1 B   2 C   3 B   4 B   5 C   6 A   7 C

## Audio script

**Presenter** Today we are pleased to welcome environmentalist Daniel James, who is going to talk about the Eden Project.
**Daniel** Good afternoon.
**Presenter** Daniel, for the benefit of those people who may not know what the Eden Project is, could you start by giving us a bit of background information?
**Daniel** Of course. The Eden Project is an environmental project in Cornwall and is one of the most popular charging visitor attractions in the UK. It opened to the general public in 2001, and averages around 2 million visitors a year both from Britain and abroad. *Amazingly, for 30% of the visitors it's their first time in Cornwall.*
**Presenter** Really? Why did they decide to build it in Cornwall?
**Daniel** It provided the perfect conditions, basically: mild climate, clean air, ample water.
**Presenter** So, for people who haven't visited the Eden Project yet, can you describe it?
**Daniel** Of course. The Project consists of two giant dome-like conservatories made up of hexagons – each approximately nine metres across – and *consisting of steel tubes covered with a very strong, transparent plastic*, which is guaranteed to last at least twenty-five years. The two domes plus a further outdoor area recreate the natural environments of three different climates, or Biomes as they are called, found around the world. The Humid Tropics Biome recreates the natural environment of the world's warmest regions. *It houses hundreds of trees and other plants from the jungles of South America, Africa, Asia and Australia*: trees like banana trees, rubber trees, cocoa, teak and mahogany. It is the largest and most impressive of the three biomes. The Warm Temperate Biome is filled with plants from the Mediterranean regions of the world – South Africa, California and the Mediterranean itself. *The third biome is the Roofless Biome. This is an open outdoor area with varied plant life from the temperate Cornwall area, as well as similar climates in Chile, the Himalayas, Asia and Australia.*
**Presenter** Fascinating! But why did they decide to build it?
**Daniel** It's not, as many people might think, to preserve plants and trees which are threatened with extinction. No, *it's primarily to demonstrate the important relationship between us and plant life; our inter-dependence, if you like.*
**Presenter** I see and is the Project aimed at anyone in particular?
**Daniel** Well, *it particularly hopes to interest the fifty-three million Britons who are not particularly concerned about the environment* rather than the three million who are already members of environmental groups, though obviously it welcomes them as well.
**Presenter** So finally, for people who are thinking of visiting, when is the best time to come?
**Daniel** It's best either to arrive first thing – around 9 a.m. – or after 2.30, when things are a little quieter. *From research carried out over the past few months, it seems the average stay is between three and four hours. There are about ninety exhibits, so just four minutes spent at each of them would be 360 minutes, or six hours. Even then you will probably wish to return another day to take it all in.*
**Presenter** Thank you, Daniel. And now …. (fade)

## Vocabulary page 53

1 a to    f about, to
   b in    g against
   c on    h on
   d to    i to, between
   e in    j to

2 a make, with    f takes, for
   b making, from    g take, in
   c take, off    h make, of
   d make, for    i take, at
   e made, with

## Reading and Use of English

page 55

1 D   2 C   3 A   4 B   5 C   6 B

## Vocabulary page 55

1 observation / observer, prediction, definition, explanation, reaction, variation / variety, behaviour, performance / performer, occurrence, suggestion, fluctuation, eruption

## Grammar page 56

1 a Non-defining: The word 'smog', which was coined in the early 20th century, combines the words 'smoke' and 'fog'.
   b Non-defining: In the late 19th century, London, which was known as 'The Big Smoke', suffered almost constant foggy conditions.
   c Defining
   d Defining
   e Non-defining: Because of the poor visibility, which was often less than one metre, dozens died in road accidents.
   f Non-defining: These days smog, which particularly affects people who have respiratory problems, is mainly caused when fuel emissions from cars react with sunlight in humid, still, atmospheric conditions.
   g Defining
   h Defining
   i Defining

2 a The 10.05 from London to Norwich, which is due to arrive at Platform 1, will call at Colchester, Ipswich and Norwich.
   b We'll have the party next Friday, which is the day when / that he comes out of hospital.
   c The golden eagle, whose eggs are stolen by unscrupulous collectors, is now an endangered species.
   d What's the name of the girl who / that got married to Chris Small? Is it Louise?
   e Can you think of any reason why he might have done it?
   f I don't know of any restaurants where you can get a decent meal for under £15.
   g What's the name of that singer whose record was number one last month? The one who / that writes his own songs.
   h United's second goal, which was scored in the final minute, won them the cup.
   i Sally's going out with someone who / that she met at Jason's party.
   j Not surprisingly, we never got back the things which / that we'd reported stolen.
   k We'll be staying at the Seaview Hotel, which is on the seafront.
   l The best time to go to Scotland is June, when the weather is warmer.
   m I've decided I don't like the shoes which / that I bought on Saturday.
   n The Hilton is expensive, which is what you'd expect. After all, it is a five-star hotel.
   o The girl over there who / that is talking to John used to go to my school.

3 Sentences e, i, j, m

4 a The guest house we stayed at when we were in Prague was right in the city centre.
   b The couple we shared our table at lunch with were from Poland. / The couple we shared our table with at lunch were from Poland.
   c The travel agency we booked our holiday through was excellent.
   d The tour, which we had heard so much about, was definitely worth going on.
   e The audio guide, which we would have been lost without, was available in several languages.
   f The holiday we'd looked forward to so much was over too soon.

## Reading and Use of English

page 57

1   1 international    5 sight
   2 medical    6 strengthening
   3 donation    7 blindness
   4 knowledge    8 treatment

## Writing page 57

1 a If parking in the town centre were made more expensive, people might be encouraged to leave their cars at home.
   b A park-and-ride scheme could be introduced. A car park could be built outside the town with cheap parking, and free transport could be provided into the town centre.
   c More bicycle racks, where bikes can be left safely, should be installed.
   d Cars could be banned from going into the town centre altogether and only bikes, taxis and buses (be) allowed.
   e If the suggested changes were implemented, the amount of pollution in the town centre would be reduced.

# Unit 10

## Reading and Use of English

page 59

1 D   2 A   3 B   4 C   5 D   6 A
7 C   8 B   9 B   10 C

## Vocabulary page 59

1   1 a dessert    b desert
   2 a compliment    b complement
   3 a stationary    b stationery
   4 a effect    b affect
   5 a economical    b economic
   6 a principle    b principal

2 a on    d off
   b off    e up
   c with    f up

3 a gamble    e advice
   b blame    f dislike
   c interest    g offence
   d seat

## Grammar page 60

1 a had
   b hadn't gone
   c could
   d would put

e  had remembered
f  didn't live
g  had worked, (had) got
h  hadn't eaten
i  were / was
j  would hurry up
k  hadn't got married
l  would stop
m  had learned
n  had listened

2  a  go
   b  ate
   c  play
   d  have
   e  didn't invite
   f  called
   g  drive
   h  not arrive
   i  visited

3  a  to get up.
   b  you got your own place
   c  to / you put the lamb in the oven
   d  you had a holiday

## Reading and Use of English

page 61

1  wish you had told
2  would rather you didn't
3  don't regret choosing / don't regret having chosen
4  have been several complaints
5  made up your mind
6  took off on time despite

## Vocabulary  page 62

1  a  made up for
   b  make it up to
   c  made their spare bedroom into
   d  make out
   e  made up

2  a  hearted
   b  short
   c  headed
   d  looking
   e  easy
   f  sweet
   g  far
   h  tanned
   i  thick
   j  fashioned
   k  see
   l  ready

| R | K | Z | S | W | E | E | T | P | R | S | E | E |
|---|---|---|---|---|---|---|---|---|---|---|---|---|
| J | E | W | H | E | A | D | E | D | S | C | X | L |
| S | F | O | O | D | L | O | O | K | I | N | G | A |
| E | F | A | S | H | I | O | N | E | D | M | O | T |
| A | J | I | R | F | T | R | E | T | C | H | Y | A |
| S | C | G | E | A | I | E | K | H | R | A | C | N |
| Y | M | I | A | R | Y | E | T | I | O | R | O | N |
| E | Q | N | D | I | N | H | B | C | E | D | L | E |
| K | I | A | Y | A | E | F | I | K | V | U | D | D |
| A | O | L | I | L | C | R | S | H | O | R | T | E |
| H | E | A | R | T | E | D | Y | E | B | D | A | S |

3  a  innovative
   b  successful
   c  affordable
   d  artistic
   e  Numerous

## Listening  page 63

1  two people
2  (fixed) wing
3  a straight line
4  expensive
5  the (British) weather
6  conventional
7  rounder
8  traffic jams
9  a long time
10  practical use

### Audio script

The way we get about has a profound impact on the way we live – affecting where we set up home, work and holiday. So, looking into the future, what changes might come about in the way we get around? What big ideas are out there, and do they have any chance of seeing the light of day?

Well, one big idea is flying cars. So what will they be like? How will they work? Well, they will have closed cabins, heating, stereos and *enough room for two people.* You'll take off from a field or a runway near your home and be able to fly to towns and cities across the country. *After you land, you'll detach the fixed wing from your vehicle and continue your journey by road* – right up to your final destination – just as if you were travelling by car. The engines will be very fuel-efficient so they'll be cheaper to run than the cars we use now, and *there will be less impact on the environment as you'll be able to go in a straight line from A to B* rather than on winding roads, as is often the case now.

But will flying cars really happen? Well, it's certainly a possibility. One microlight firm is already building closed-cabin vehicles, and some of these can fly for up to four hours. *And they will not necessarily be very expensive.* A combined three-wheel car and microlight could cost about £30,000 at today's prices.

However, like everything, *there are some downsides. The main one, in Britain at any rate, will be the weather.* The British weather often prevents microlight flying, and you can only travel during daylight hours. Also, you need an airfield nearby. *But flying cars won't mean an end to*

*conventional cars. I'm sure we'll still use them,* but the car of the future will be more environmentally-friendly and much safer. Engines could be powered by a waste-fuelled reactor. Alternatively, petrol may be replaced by fuel cells, which combine hydrogen and oxygen. The design will probably be different, too. *Cars will be rounder* and they will have sensors to detect pedestrians and other cars and have air cushions both inside and out. They may also run along invisible tracks, via satellite technology. *Traffic flow could even be controlled with vehicles 'talking' to each other to regulate flow – so no more traffic jams.* I'm sure that twenty years from now we will see examples on our roads.

However, so many millions of people own cars that *it'll be a long time before environmental and safety improvements become commonplace.* The technology is still experimental and it remains to be seen whether car firms are willing to invest in this. *Finally, people always ask me about jet packs* as used by James Bond in the film *Thunderball.* Well, I'm sorry to disappoint everyone, but *it's looking increasingly unlikely that they will ever feature as a future mode of travel. And it's simply because it remains difficult to build a cheap, reliable version which has a practical use.* They're handy for retrieving cats from trees, cleaning hard-to-reach windows and arriving in style at a party, but not much else, I'm afraid.

## Writing  page 63

1  1  described
   2  large
   3  gives
   4  appears
   5  compulsive
   6  opening to closing
   7  assure

2  a  novelist
   b  autobiography
   c  plot
   d  chapter
   e  fictional

# Unit 11

## Listening  page 64

1
1 B   2 C   3 A   4 B   5 A   6 C
7 A   8 C

## Audio script

**1**

**Woman** I think the British use more gestures than they used to. It may be partly because we come into contact with other nationalities more often than in the past – you know, on foreign holidays, or when we see foreigners on television. I think we've got used to seeing people gesturing, and we've started doing it ourselves. I remember *when I was a child I thought anyone who moved their hands and arms about when they were talking was very odd.* Now I'd say it's much more common.

**2**

**Int** Do you think you could tell us something about how you learned Thai?

**Man** Of course. It was when I was working as a teacher in Bangkok.

**Int** Did you have lessons or did you just pick it up?

**Man** Both. I lived with a Thai family, and I also went to evening classes at a local college.

**Int** Did the family teach you?

**Man** Not exactly, but I certainly learned from them. Even though they could speak English very well, *I insisted that they always spoke to me in Thai. That way I was forced to use the language.*

**Int** And the evening classes?

**Man** They helped of course, but I found the grammar quite difficult.

**3**

**Woman** I've known Maggie since we were at school together. We've met regularly ever since. One year she'll come and stay with me, and the next I'll visit her. And we've had a few holidays together. *And on top of that we've always written regular letters.* We've been doing it now for over forty years. We've only ever missed a couple of letters: once when I was away on holiday and once when Maggie was in hospital having one of her children. We've thought about changing to the phone or email, but there's something very special about writing old-fashioned letters.

**4**

**Man** And remember, when you're answering the interviewer's questions, look them in the eye.

**Woman** I find it quite difficult to keep eye contact for longer than a few seconds. I feel quite embarrassed.

**Man** You need to practise doing it. *Obviously, you've got to be careful not to look as if you're staring*, so that means not opening your eyes too wide.

**Woman** What about blinking? Is it OK to blink?

**Man** Yes, of course. It's not some kind of competition to see who's the first to blink. It's just a way of showing that you're interested in the person you're talking to.

**5**

**Man** I wouldn't say I'm a particularly honest person – it's just that I'm just not very good at lying. I can still remember the first lie I ever told. I was about six at the time. I had some medicine for a sore throat and I hated the taste of it. My mother promised she'd take me shopping as soon as I'd had this horrible medicine. So I hid the medicine at the back of a cupboard and told my mother I'd taken it. *About five minutes after we got back from the shops my mother found it.* She wasn't angry – just really upset. I'll never forget the look on her face.

**6**

**Woman** It was awful – I just didn't know what to do.

**Man** Didn't you have your mobile with you?

**Woman** Yes, I did, but the battery was flat.

**Man** What about the emergency phones? There's usually one of those about every 500 metres.

**Woman** I could probably have reached one, but I was worried about leaving the car and walking around outside on my own. And it was rush hour – the road was incredibly busy.

**Man** So what did you do?

**Woman** I just waited and hoped someone would stop and help me. *The thing is, I've never changed a tyre before.* Eventually, thank goodness, a police car stopped.

**7**

**Woman** I took early retirement from work because of illness and decided to do a course in creative writing at our local university. It was just for fun, really – and to keep myself occupied – *I never thought I'd get anything published.* The course lasted two years and towards the end they invited a number of literary agents to meet us. During the second year, I wrote the first draft of a story connected with my family and one of the agents seemed interested. We met a couple more times and he decided to take me on. And the rest, as they say, is history. My second novel's coming out next month.

**8**

**Woman** We're open every day except Sundays.

**Man** *OK – and how do I become a member?*

**Woman** If you complete this form and bring it back here, we'll issue you a card.

**Man** And what does that entitle me to?

**Woman** It allows you to use all of our facilities and to take out three books at a time for up to two weeks.

**Man** And can I access the internet here?

**Woman** Yes, we have a computer suite on the first floor.

**Man** Great! And how much is all this?

**Woman** At the moment, there's no charge if you live locally, but there may be a fee for internet usage in the future.

**Man** Thank you very much.

## Vocabulary page 64

1  a  stuck up for
   b  stick together
   c  stuck at
   d  stick by
   e  sticking to
   f  sticking out of

2  a  said          d  told
   b  tell          e  speak
   c  speak         f  talking

3  a N   b P   c N   d N   e N   f N
   g P

4  b  lazy              e  overconfident
   c  well-built        f  cold
   d  cheap             g  determined

5  a  expect / am expecting, hope
   b  wait
   c  looking forward to
   d  is expecting, waiting
   e  hope
   f  looking forward to, wait

## Reading and Use of English

page 67

1 E   2 G   3 B   4 D   5 A   6 F
Extra sentence: C

## Vocabulary page 67

1  b  beauty
   c  fame
   d  hostility
   e  nationality / nation
   f  reality / realism
   g  superiority
   h  terror
2  b  conclusion
   c  conviction
   d  disappearance
   e  existence
   f  indication / indicator
   g  observation / observer
   h  suggestion

## Reading and Use of English

page 67

1  such          5  been
2  it            6  from / at
3  not           7  that / which
4  as            8  to

## Grammar page 68

1  a  will go
   b  takes
   c  wouldn't look
   d  will tell

   e  wouldn't have stopped
   f  is
   g  wouldn't have got
   h  hasn't got
   i  will phone
   j  practised

2  a  If Sue hadn't been ill, she would
       have gone to the party. / Sue
       would have gone to the party if she
       hadn't been ill.
   b  If there was a theatre in my town,
       I'd go (to the theatre) more often. /
       I'd go to the theatre more often if
       there was one in my town.
   c  If Jeff hadn't broken his leg, he
       could have played football. / Jeff
       could have played football if he
       hadn't broken his leg.
   d  If my mother wasn't afraid of water,
       she would go swimming. / My
       mother would go swimming if she
       wasn't afraid of water.
   e  If I had £100,000 to spare, I'd buy
       a yacht. / I'd buy a yacht if I had
       £100,000 to spare.
   f  If it had snowed, we could have
       gone skiing. / We could have gone
       skiing if it had snowed.
   g  If I knew her address, I could send
       her a postcard. / I could send her
       a postcard if I knew her address.
   h  If he'd been looking where he was
       going, he wouldn't have walked into
       the road sign. / He wouldn't have
       walked into the road sign if he'd
       been looking where he was going.

3  a  unless        d  provided that
   b  as long as    e  Unless
   c  If

## Writing page 69

1  A 3   B 1   C 4   D 2
2  A 3 f   B 1 h   C 4 e   D 2 g

# Unit 12

## Listening page 70

1 D   2 G   3 H   4 A   5 C
Extra sentences: B, E, F

### Audio script

**Speaker 1**
I live on a council estate. It's not like
it used to be. Now there are all these
gangs and drug-dealing and the like, and
quite honestly *I'm scared to go out on my
own after dark. And I'm not the only one*

*who feels like this. People feel trapped
in their homes.* Just last month my
neighbour had his pension stolen when
he was walking home in broad daylight.
These two young girls pushed him and
stole his money. He still hasn't got over
it. *He hasn't been out of his house once
since it happened.* I'm not sure what the
answer is. Should we punish the children
or punish the parents? I don't know.

**Speaker 2**
A lot of people blame the parents. But
I'm a parent myself and I know how hard
it is nowadays to bring up a child. It can
be particularly hard if you're a single
mother and you've got boys. Once they're
past the age of ten, they don't pay any
attention to you; and if there isn't a man
around to lay down the law, well then
they just do what they want. *I don't think
parents can be held responsible for what
their kids get up to, but I think they should
set a good example, lay down rules, and
try to make their kids stick to those rules,
but that's all they can do.*

**Speaker 3**
I was shocked when the police came
round and told us that they'd got our
Wayne down at the station. I couldn't
believe it when they said he'd been
caught stealing sweets from a shop.
He's always been a good lad. Never
been in any trouble before. When I
asked him why he'd done it, he said that
all his mates were doing it. It was just a
dare. He said he knew it was wrong and
he was sorry but I'm just worried he'll
do it again. *It's hard not to just follow the
crowd. That's why a lot of kids get into
trouble, isn't it? They're not really bad,
just easily influenced.*

**Speaker 4**
You can't let them just get away with it!
There are kids of seven or eight on the
estate where I live. They go round in
gangs of twenty or thirty. They start off
doing things like smashing phone boxes
and breaking people's windows, but it
isn't long before they graduate to bigger
things like stealing cars and selling drugs.
The problem is that the police can't do
much about it when they're young. They
just caution them and send them home.
*But I think they should be made to pay
for what they do. I don't necessarily mean
they should be locked up, but something
should definitely be done.*

**Speaker 5**

*You have to realize that these young people haven't got much money and so there is a limited number of things they can do.* They can't afford to go to the cinema or go bowling, or at least not very often. They are too young to go to pubs or nightclubs. They want to be with other young people their own age, but they don't want to be stuck at home. So what do they do? Hang about in the street, meet up with other young people and get into trouble quite simply because they are bored.

## Reading and Use of English

page 70

1  1 D   2 A   3 E   4 B   5 E   6 B
   7 C   8 A   9 C   10 D

## Vocabulary  page 72

1  a  arrested, shoplifting
   b  burglary, burgled
   c  speeding, drink-driving
   d  hooligans
   e  mugger
   f  vandalism

2  a  committing, arrested, charged
   b  court, bail, trial, trial
   c  jury, verdict, guilty, guilty
   d  judge, probation, committed, sentence, death penalty

3  a  fill it up
   b  tore the letter up
   c  wrapped up
   d  drink up
   e  tidy it up
   f  Eat up
   g  clear up

## Reading and Use of English

page 73

1  1 household      5 achievement
   2 disposable     6 possession(s)
   3 financial      7 unwanted
   4 equipment      8 functional

## Writing  page 73

1  a  Both older people and many young people are scared to go into the town centre at night.
   b  As the bars and clubs are open until late, some people end up drinking too much.
   c  As well as becoming argumentative, some people get into fights.

   d  In addition to increasing the number of police officers on the street, more CCTV cameras should be installed and linked directly to the police station.
   e  Buses should run throughout the night so that people wouldn't have to walk home.
   f  Not only would these improvements make our town a safer place to be at night but also a more pleasant place to be (at night).

## Grammar  page 74

1  a  could / might have
   b  she can't be / mustn't be
   c  I might
   d  must have taken
   e  can't have been / might not have been / must not have been
   f  It must be
   g  I could / might be
   h  You must have
   i  we must have
   j  You might not have given him
   k  She could / might / must be
   l  It could / might / must be

2  a  can't          d  can't
   b  can't          e  could
   c  may

3  a  the
   b  A / The, the, the
   c  The
   d  a, an, Ø
   e  a, the, the, a
   f  a, a
   g  Ø, the, the
   h  The, the, Ø, the

4  a  a (6)          f  Ø, Ø (9)
   b  The, the (10)  g  Ø, Ø (7)
   c  an (1)         h  Ø, the (2)
   d  Ø, Ø, Ø (8)    i  a (5)
   e  an, a (3)      j  a, Ø (4)

## Vocabulary  page 75

1  a  got away with
   b  is / was getting on
   c  didn't get on
   d  get away
   e  get me down
   f  got by
   g  get over
   h  got out

key

## What is on the Workbook MultiROM?

The MultiROM in this Workbook Pack has two parts.

- You can listen to the audio material that accompanies the workbook by playing the MultiROM in an audio CD player, or in a media player on your computer.

- You can also access a complete practice test online with the MultiROM. The test comes with instant marking, feedback, tips, a dictionary look-up, and many other features. To find out how to access the test, read this page.

## How do I use my MultiROM?

You will find your practice test on a website called oxfordenglishtesting.com. The website contains many different practice tests, including the one that you have access to. Because the practice test is on the internet you will need:
- to be connected to the internet when you use the test
- to have an email address (so that you can register).

When you're ready to try out your practice test for the first time follow these steps:
1  Turn on your computer.
2  Connect to the internet. (If you have a broadband connection, you will probably already be online.)

3  Put the MultiROM into the CD drive of your computer.
4  A screen will appear giving you two options. Single click to access your test.

## What do I do when I get to the website?

After a few moments your internet browser will open and take you directly to the Welcome page on the website. Follow the steps below.

1  Choose a language from the drop-down list and click **Go**. All pages, apart from the actual practice test, will be in the language you choose.

2  Click on the **Register now** button and fill in the details on the registration form. You will need to give an email address and make up a password. You will need your email address and password every time you log into the system. If you are already registered, click on the **Log in** button.

3  After filling in the registration form click on **Register**. To confirm your registration, click on **Save registration details**. Click on **My tests** where you will be asked to log in. You have 365 days to use the practice test before you have to submit it for final marking.

4  If you have a problem using your MultiROM, go to www.oxfordenglishtesting.com/unlock. You will be asked to click **Register now** if you are a new user. You will then be asked to fill in a registration form and to enter an unlock code. You can find the unlock code printed on your MultiROM. It will look like this 9219e6-9471d9-cf7c79-a5143b. Each code is unique.

Once you have registered, you can access your test in future by going to oxfordenglishtesting.com and logging in. Remember you will need your email and password to log in. You must also be online to do your practice test.